# Punting Poverty

by Damon Dunn

Punting Poverty: Breaking the Chains of Welfare
By Damon Dunn
May 2020

ISBN: 978-1-934276-42-6

Pacific Research Institute
101 Montgomery Street, Suite 1300
San Francisco, CA 94104
Tel: 415-989-0833
Fax: 415-989-2411
www.pacificresearch.org

# Punting Poverty
## Breaking the Chains of Welfare

by Damon Dunn

*I dedicate this book to my mom, Ramona Williams. She was the first person in our family to go college, move up the socioeconomic ladder and end poverty for all future generations of our family. Mom, thank you for showing me that education was our way up and our way out of poverty and for leading me into a relationship with Christ. I love you with all my heart. Damon*

# TABLE OF CONTENTS

# FOREWORD

As I sit here working in my living room writing this, we are in the midst of a global pandemic. Millions of people around the world have tested positive for the novel coronavirus (COVID-19). In the United States alone, over 1.2 million people have tested positive and over 73,000 have died. We are in uncertain times and uncharted territory. With nonessential businesses shut down, and Americans required to self-quarantine, I'm given the opportunity to reflect on what are the constants in our lives and where can we find security. Of course, family, faith and friends come first to mind. They are the rocks that guide us all in times like these.

Looking further down the road when the dust has settled and we all get back to a somewhat more normal life, at the top of my mind is an important question – what is it that will matter? Here Damon Dunn's book lays out the path that will liberate so many of us.

We can't rely on government handouts to solve all our problems. For those of us who come from economically challenged backgrounds, our true path to upward economic mobility is an education coupled with real economic opportunity. Equally compelling is Damon's take on a new safety net that vests us all into America's long-term economic success.

My story isn't much different than Damon's, and I hope my future is as bright. I was raised in South Central Los Angeles by my mother, Carol Riley who sacrificed her life for me. She worked full-time as a cafeteria worker at an aerospace company and years later as a janitor at UCLA. She barely had enough money after paying the necessary bills to take care of the household. My father left me when I was less than three years old and never provided any support to my mother toward fulfilling our daily needs.

I did receive help from the government and it did help round out the edges, but to be dependent on it only limits one's future, not magnifies it. My mother prioritized for me so that I could attend California State University, Long Beach. The hard work in the classroom allowed me to graduate and secure my first job at the City of Long Beach in the Transportation Engineering Division. The job meant more to me than just a paycheck. It started my career and my path towards building wealth. I was able to make enough income to move into my own place and to start building wealth by saving surplus income and investing in real estate rentals.

Looking back, government may have lent a hand, but it was an education, hard work and opportunity that changed my life. Looking ahead, it will be the same. When all this uncertainty passes, we will need real economic opportunities more than ever, and education will be the key to seizing those opportunities when they come.

Kevin Dewayne Riley
Graduate of Cal State Long Beach
City Transportation Engineer, City of Beverly Hills

# CHAPTER ONE
## My Path to Economic Freedom

The taste of mayonnaise and white bread for dinner still sits on the tip of my tongue even to this day…thirty years later. Looking back now, my childhood doesn't seem so bad. At the time, I did not understand how poor we were. But we were poor enough to only eat mayonnaise sandwiches for dinner toward the end of every month when our government assistance had been exhausted.

I was raised by my grandparents, two wonderful people who loved and cared for me and my five uncles after my mother went off to get a college education and start a career. Only years later would I realize what sacrifices my mother made and how making her own way to independence would pave the way for my own economic freedom.

We lived in rural Texas outside Fort Worth in a single wide trailer. My grandfather made just enough money, either by design or luck, to qualify for all the government assistance that was available. From food stamps and welfare to free government cheese and Medicaid, we were the working poor to whom the promise of socialism should have been captivating.

I watched extended family—aunts and uncles, nieces and nephews—struggle in the same way. They were born poor and died poor despite billions in government assistance offered to them and people like them. The well-intentioned government programs often championed by progressives at best eased daily life but never produced the upward economic mobility people needed to change their lives.

Today's leading progressive voices, whether they be Alexandria Ocasio-Cortez or Andrew Yang, may be well intentioned at best, opportunists at worst, but more likely just misguided. Their socialist rhetoric from universal basic income to Medicaid for All ignores the simple fact that people just want to live independent and prosperous lives.

> **In offering government welfare as the solution, they offer no upward mobility and no economic freedom.**

Indeed, wherever socialism has advanced, it has failed to increase economic mobility, raise standards of living, and enhance the quality of life of the people. In fact, it has reversed these standards. And even worse, it has often led to totalitarianism. Old and new examples of socialism from world history start with the promise of prosperity and freedom and end with stagnation and servitude.

Socialism as advocated today by Elizabeth Warren and Bernie Sanders is the new slavery. These leftist leaders promote public policies that drive up the cost of living and keep people poor forever. In offering government welfare as the solution, they offer no upward mobility and no economic freedom. Their policies permanently enslave poor people and lock them out of America's historic promise of a better life.

Is Mark Zuckerberg teaching his kids that the best they can expect in life is a government handout? No. And no parent should. Otherwise, we will doom our children to a life enslaved by government-imposed limits. How is this any different than a life enslaved by a master? The outcome is the same, only the master is different. In this instance the master – big government – offers what appears to be the best of intentions. Never mind that it always over promises and under delivers. And when big government inevitably fails, it doubles down and further tightens its grip on power, choking away ever more of our freedoms.

The road to modern day slavery is paved with good intentions. This book will advance the reforms that not only will provide people with upward economic mobility but the freedom that accompanies being able to take care of oneself and one's family.

The path forward for working poor people is not more government promising everything for free, it is real empowerment through education and opportunity. Government must create the conditions that help people learn and acquire new skills. Economic policies should focus on growing and creating more wealth for all.

My personal story is the perfect example. We lived on government support and stayed poor for as long as we relied on those programs. We gamed the system; maintained our eligibility; and survived on the bare minimum that ensured access to every free program possible. But in the end, we did not find economic freedom until my mother got her degree, secured a good job, and paved the way for me to do the same.

My path came through school and sports. I still remember the day our middle school janitor passed me in the hallway. I had been dismissed from class for being a troublemaker and distracting other students. I thought I was funny. In just one minute that janitor changed my life. He said, "Look back inside at the white students. They'll be your bosses one day if you don't get your act together." I'd never get out, I'd always be poor, and nothing would change for me. He was right.

With my mom as my inspiration and with the sacrifices of my grandparents, I excelled in school and developed my athletic skills on the football field. An All-American high school wide receiver, I got a full ride football scholarship to Stanford University. My life was changed forever. I went on to a four-year career in professional football and the NFL, and then started a successful real estate development company.

The path to freedom is not accepting the limits of government handouts. The path to freedom is developing marketable skills and seizing opportunities. This is a formula that can be repeated by anyone and at any time if government focuses its efforts, not on free handouts that make economic suffering tolerable, but truly equips people to thrive and prosper.

> The path to freedom is not accepting the limits of government handouts. The path to freedom is developing marketable skills and seizing opportunities.

What does this look like? Schools that offer options for both academic success and vocational training. A government that promotes economic opportunity. A growing economy that offers meaningful work to skilled workers and the well-educated. Government policies that don't punish work and drive up the cost of living but empower working-class people to afford housing, educate their children, find accessible health care, and save for retirement.

This book lays out my journey, questions the traditional progressive approach, and promotes a new way of empowering and equipping people to take care of themselves. It is dense with data and facts because future public policy decisions, especially as grand and far-reaching as those proposed by the socialists of our era, deserve the rigor of data and evidence-based analysis, not sweeping rhetoric.

There are those who want to remake the debate over poverty and incomes into one based on the politics of identity. It is not.

That trailer from my youth was in a rural, mainly white community. My mother moved us to an African-American neighborhood in Dallas. The struggles in both areas—the more conservative rural area and the more liberal urban—were the same. The debilitating effects coming from dependence on government assistance were the same. The potential futures shaped by a lifetime of learning to live by government rules were the same.

The poor were expected to require assistance. They were expected to strip themselves of assets required to build a better future in order to get government aid. They were expected to qualify only for minimum wage jobs. Training came from government workers and government contractors who expected the poor to land low-wage jobs, low hours, and low benefits. Children grew up watching their parents, grandparents, and neighbors in this system, and expected to do the same.

Most people do not want to live a life on government assistance, and those that rely on these programs want to get off. People want a helping hand when they need it most but the current system is instead designed to trap them into a life of dependency.

Today, the poor are not confined to a physical almshouse, but instead a figurative one built from government rules.

Too many of my peers lacked the kind of encouragement my mother gave me. The hope for the future was in what one had to do to keep the government assistance coming. And as the programs continued to expand, what one had to do to get in line for those benefits as well. Counseling for the future was not so much about what you had to do to get a job or what educational and skill paths could get you to a decent or better wage. Rather, it was social workers, county workers, community organizers, and helpful neighbors walking you through the forms and rules.

For those who shot for something higher, rather than work or building a business, the role model was the chimera of rappers and others who magically achieved overnight success or through crime or drugs. The media—traditional media in the beginning years and social media in the latter—did little more than confirm these models in their minds. Lessons learned by watching those around them left little room for anything else.

We all try to live up to our expectations. Getting more people out of poverty and moving people up the economic ladder means we also have to try to raise them as well.

In thirty years, I went from eating mayonnaise sandwiches to eating whatever might be pleasing. There were hard days and nights of work. It wasn't easy and it came not just with my sacrifices but those of my mother and grandparents. It was a generational transition and, God willing, my family will never be dependent on government again.

# CHAPTER TWO
## The Paradox of Poverty

Looking back over my life and thinking about the outcomes of myself and my peers, one thing stands out. While all of us experienced the same social environment of broken homes, crime, bad schools, gangs, high unemployment, and lack of opportunity, there was one big difference between my peers and me: expectations.

My mother was the first person in our family to go to college. She came back for me when I was eleven years old and she established the expectation of college in my life. She associated college with success. Through her example and her daily encouragement to study hard, she passed this expectation on to my sister and me, opening a new world of economic opportunities for the first time in our family's saga.

Most of my peers did not have someone at home encouraging them to set the same high expectations and the public schools did little more than confirm their poor prospects in life. Their default became what they saw their parents and their neighbors doing, relying on welfare programs.

Once they settled for welfare, a vicious cycle began. Eligibility typically requires an applicant to meet strict income requirements and, in some programs, asset limits as well. Any effort to improve their lot in life came at a cost as they became ineligible for the benefits. By being in the welfare and assistance system, they grew to know what they needed to do to keep the benefits coming. Intermittent employment at low and no-skill jobs meant they gained no comparable experience in how to maneuver within the working world or what they needed to do to position themselves for a good job and increasing wages. Their lives became shaped by the incentives to maintain a lifestyle of poverty, with no motivation for economic empowerment. They drew these expectations from the lessons of their parents, grandparents, and peers. Many have passed them on to their children as well.

My family lived within this quandary. My grandfathers each worked all their lives. Combined with what my grandmothers brought in from part-time jobs, our families earned enough that they did not have to resort to AFDC (Aid to Families with Dependent Children), but still fell within the income cutoff for the food assistance essential to rounding out the monthly budget. But even for them, getting off government assistance didn't mean just earning enough to rise above the income standard. It meant earning enough to replace what my family would have lost in benefits and then earning some more to get to where we would actually come out ahead. It didn't mean earning 5 percent more a month; it meant earning an additional 10 to 20 percent or more when taxes came into play. Neither grandfather had the skills to justify getting that pay, and both were a little too old to go back to school and get them—even if our family could have afforded for them to take the time off.

One night, my grandmother sat at the kitchen table and, as she did every month, ran through the family's budget numbers. My grandfather was in line for a small raise and she was hoping to get one at her part-time job as well. But rather than rejoice at finally having a little extra money to buy more than just the bare necessities, her calculations showed that we would end up further behind. Their incomes combined would put us above the line for the food benefits, but factoring in taxes, we would be left worse off than before. With great reluctance and no small loss to her sense of self-worth, my grandmother decided that she had no choice but to quit her job. The family's needs were more important to her than her own.

She gave up more than her job that night; she also gave up part of her future. She could have used that extra money to help save for retirement, an education, perhaps even moving out of that trailer. Giving up that job also meant reducing Social Security when and if she finally retired—the one government program that really promised to do some good when she would need it the most. But retirement was in the future. Ten hungry mouths to feed were in the here and now.

My grandmother's actions taught me a lesson that night, the wrong one until it was replaced by the higher hopes brought back by my mother. My uncles were sitting at that table as well, and the lesson they learned instead was one they would carry through their lives. They remain poor and dependent on government assistance to this day.

The poverty programs did not "cure" poverty. Instead, they have worked to cement it in place.

# THE BALKANIZATION OF POVERTY PROGRAMS

The current structure of public assistance programs has been cobbled together over time so that the exact count is now up for debate. The Congressional Research Service estimates that there are 102 separate federal programs.[1] The Washington, D.C.-based Heritage Foundation estimates cover 93 different programs.[2]

Federal anti-poverty efforts list 104 programs for economic, community, and regional development based on the current Catalog of Federal Domestic Assistance[3]. A search for training programs brings up 599 different ones. While not all are broadly available, or are targeted for job creation and poverty issues, these numbers illustrate how a basic concept – the need to help the poor out of poverty, exploded into hundreds of bureaucratic and often competing divisions.

Each of these programs carries its associated rules and standards for eligibility based on income, family composition, asset levels, and so on. Food stamp eligibility alone takes into account more than a dozen factors. These rules change over time, both at the federal and state levels. Funding and the degree of benefits vary, subject to economic cycles, political shifts, and budget capacity. Qualifying for benefits does not always mean receiving them right away. Housing vouchers, for example, may mean getting in line for years.

States and communities spend considerable resources and sometimes resort to litigation to ensure they remain within the constraints of the rules stipulated in their federal grants. Yet the poor and the working poor, with no access to this knowledge base, are somehow expected on their own to know, understand, and fully comply.

The fact is they don't. In a California research project component conducted by the research firm Vision Strategy and Insights, only 54 percent of respondents in the survey of working poor believed they were probably or definitely receiving all the benefits from public assistance programs to which they were entitled. Nearly a third considered the qualification processes to be difficult.[4] The effort required to maintain eligibility for just one program is more than enough for most families.

This situation runs counter to the basic tenet of the nation's anti-poverty efforts as originally devised. The programs were intended to assist the poor in working their way out of poverty. Yet, basic financial decision-making and planning is impossible if the rules are always changing or are too complex to understand. Families on assistance must cope with this uncertainty, not knowing from month to month whether the benefits on which they depend will continue, or whether those few hours of overtime will put them over the income limit or force them to pay some of the benefits back. For a household on assistance, it is hard to figure out how to work your way out of the system if you do not know which step will inadvertently put you outside of it before you are financially ready.

This is a system that is run for the system's sake. Lacking a means of coordinating aid, rules, or even purpose, the system has become what it is—a multitude of programs that measure success by how many remain on the rolls (both positive and negative depending on the program, presidential administration, and year). Even if viewed as the de facto income redistribution system it has become, it is hard to imagine a more inefficient and inconsistent way to do it.

## THE COST OF PROGRAM DEPENDENCE

One of the important aspects of the marginal tax concept is the effect on work incentives. As marginal taxes rise, workers receive less in disposable income for additional work effort. In response, they may work fewer hours, pass on the opportunity to work more, or cease working altogether.

This is not a difficult concept, but proposals for ever higher tax rates pretend it does not exist. The many assistance programs were put in place assuming the poor would never catch on.

Historically, marginal tax rates were affected by two factors: income tax rates that increase as income grows and payroll taxes which remain level over an initial income range, then drop to zero. Now with the expansion of the various assistance programs, effective tax rates rise as cash and noncash benefits are phased out either abruptly or gradually depending on the program, drop as refundable and other tax credits become available, and then rise again as those credits are also phased out according to income.

The marginal tax rates associated with some of the means-tested assistance, food stamps (Supplemental Nutrition Assistance Program or SNAP), tax credits (Earned Income Tax Credit or EITC), and health insurance subsidies (Affordable Care Act or ACA) were estimated by the Congressional Budget Office for the years 2012 and 2016.[5] Through specific case studies covering means-tested programs, the 2012 report estimated the marginal tax rates faced by a single parent with one child seeking to move from dependence, on assistance, to work. The resulting marginal tax rate faced by that family in moving from joblessness ($0 annual earnings) to part time work ($7,540) was 36 percent. Moving from part-time to full-time work ($15,130) jumped the marginal tax rate to 47 percent.

Other analyses covering a similar but slightly wider range of assistance programs have estimated much higher rates faced by those attempting to move from dependence. A 2012 Tax Policy Center study[6] estimated that a single parent with two children would face an average marginal tax rate of 26.6 to 100 percent as they moved from the federal poverty level to 150 percent of poverty income. If earnings were instead limited to only six months of the year, the rate would drop to -17.7 to 66.0 percent on those additional earnings.

A more concrete example can be cobbled from research by the California Business Roundtable.[7] Figure 1 shows a benefit model covering the typical means-tested assistance programs as well as the value of items normally not included in social agency benefit models—notably the health care benefits.

## FIGURE 1 CALIFORNIA BENEFITS MODEL, 2022

| | SINGLE | SINGLE | SINGLE | SINGLE | SINGLE | MARRIED | MARRIED | MARRIED | MARRIED | MARRIED |
|---|---|---|---|---|---|---|---|---|---|---|
| | $10 PT | $15 PT | $20 PT/$10 FT | $15 FT | $20 FT | $10 PT | $15 PT | $20 PT/$10 FT | $15 FT | $20 FT |
| Earned Income | $10,400 | $15,600 | $20,800 | $31,200 | $41,600 | $20,800 | $31,200 | $41,600 | $62,400 | $83,200 |
| Payroll Taxes | 1,700 | 2,500 | 3,400 | 5,100 | 6,800 | 3,400 | 5,100 | 6,800 | 10,200 | 13,600 |
| Federal Income Taxes | -5,300 | -8,200 | -9,000 | -6,800 | -3,500 | -9,000 | -8,100 | -5,600 | -100 | 2,400 |
| State Income Taxes | -2,100 | -300 | -200 | 0 | 0 | -200 | 0 | 0 | 0 | 700 |
| Disposable Income | $16,100 | $21,600 | $26,600 | $32,900 | $38,300 | $26,600 | $34,200 | $40,400 | $52,300 | $66,500 |
| | | | | | | | | | | |
| **Benefit Eligibility** | | | | | | | | | | |
| TANF | $5,780 | $3,180 | $580 | $0 | $0 | $2,920 | $0 | $0 | $0 | $0 |
| SNAP | 6,600 | 6,600 | 4,120 | 0 | 0 | 5,680 | 0 | 0 | 0 | 0 |
| Childcare | 15,800 | 15,800 | 15,800 | 15,800 | 12,660 | 15,800 | 15,800 | 14,100 | 7,680 | 1,740 |
| School Lunch | 1,260 | 1,260 | 1,260 | 1,000 | 1,000 | 1,260 | 1,260 | 1,000 | 0 | 0 |
| Medicaid/CHIP | 19,500 | 19,500 | 19,500 | 19,500 | 13,000 | 26,000 | 26,000 | 13,000 | 13,000 | 0 |
| ACA Subsidy | 0 | 0 | 0 | 0 | 3,540 | 0 | 0 | 7,080 | 0 | 0 |
| Utility Subsidy | 2,050 | 2,050 | 2,050 | 2,050 | 2,140 | 2,240 | 2,240 | 2,360 | 1,480 | 0 |
| Housing Assistance | 1,150 | 1,150 | 1,150 | 1,150 | 1,150 | 1,150 | 1,150 | 1,150 | 0 | 0 |
| Total Benefit Eligibility | $52,140 | $49,540 | $44,460 | $39,500 | $33,490 | $55,050 | $46,450 | $38,690 | $22,160 | $1,740 |
| Net Income | $68,240 | $71,140 | $71,060 | $72,400 | $71,790 | $81,650 | $80,650 | $79,090 | $74,460 | $68,240 |

*Source:* All benefit eligibility amounts are based on the 2018 provisions, projected to 2022. As modified in Figure 1, the components consist of the following: 1) All values are calculated based on adjusting the California eligibility standards to their projected 2022 values. The estimates are provided for two types of families: a single parent with two children and a married couple with two children. The adults are assumed to be under 65 and without a disability or other special tax condition. The children are assumed to be under 13 for purposes of the various tax credit calculations. 2) Tax calculations have been revised in Figure 1 using TAXSIM, version 27 available through the National Bureau of Economic Research in order to reflect the federal tax reform. All income is assumed to be from wages, and both families are assumed to be renters using the average California values for their income range. Negative tax amounts reflect the effect of the refundable tax credits. 3) Cash benefits are based on the projected 2022 values. The value of noncash benefits such as housing (Section 8), Medicaid, school lunch, and childcare are based on the total program costs divided by caseload or on the maximum benefit less the available subsidy amount. Children are assumed to attend childcare full time. 4) The income levels shown cover both half-time and full-time employment at $10, $15, and $20 an hour wage. Each adult is assumed to work an equal number of hours at the same wage level.

In looking at Figure 1, two points should be emphasized. First, the benefit estimates are based on the eligible amounts for each of the model families. As discussed previously, not all eligible beneficiaries apply for every benefit, while other non-income factors may also rule them out from the start. In particular, TANF has time limits, although California applies these only to adults and not children, one of the main reasons why that state now has one-third of the total national TANF caseload.

Second, not all of the benefit amounts are available, as they assume. For example, housing assistance programs in California and other states have a significant waiting list, as does childcare. Medi-Cal (Medicaid) has also been subject to service cutbacks from both coverage and provider payment reductions. This was especially the case during the 2008-09 recession as a budget-balancing measure, with the result being that few providers were willing to take on new Medi-Cal patients.

In Figure 1, the case of the single parent shows little incentive to work more or even seek higher paying work—the net income considering both cash and noncash benefits comes out nearly the same. Greater discretionary spending does become possible as more income comes from earnings at least in theory. The more likely outcome, however, is that wages are eaten up by the costs for food, childcare, and health care that once were provided through the benefits. Extra money becomes available only if some portion of those are foregone.

The married couple, however, fares even worse. The higher their earned incomes, the lower their net income after factoring in the benefits they receive.

This model also depicts the real effect of minimum wage increases. Comparing the full-time results of $10 per hour ($20,800 annually single/$41,600 married) and $15 per hour ($31,200/$62,400), the rise mandated under current California law by 2022, shows the net disposable income effect on the single parent household is $3.03 per hour after taxes and $2.86 per hour for the married couple household.

These amounts assume their employers do not adjust to the higher costs—which, based on U.S. Bureau of Economic Analysis compensation data for 2018, works out to employer costs of $6.13 an hour on average to give that $2.86 to $3.03 hourly bump to their employees—by reducing the number of available work hours.

Both family types illustrate the point that the more government support one accepts, the higher the penalty for work or developing skills. As government assistance rises, working more or working harder at best will keep people in place, and at worse further behind.

# CHAPTER THREE
## The False Promise of Universal Basic Income

The government never "spent" my family into the middle class. Welfare programs never led to economic empowerment.

Universal Basic Income would not have done anything more to help move my family out of poverty. Giving my grandparents $500 per month would not have led to socioeconomic mobility or closed the income gap. It would not have enabled us to make a down payment to buy a home, move our family into a better neighborhood with better schools, or pay for college. At best it would have helped cover the overdue bills, enabled us to do a little better than mayonnaise sandwiches at the end of the month, and slightly upgraded the quality of clothes those of us lower in the "hand-me-down" line had to wear. It would have taken us from spending only on the absolute basic necessities and at best removed only one or two of the modifiers to that term.

Offering my family $500 per month may have made us a little more comfortable in poverty, but my grandparents still would have died poor because the hurdles to get out would have been raised even higher. Incorporating taxes, that $500 a month would have meant my grandfather would have had to go from a job paying about $5 an hour to one paying $8.94-an-hour just to stay whole and escape welfare—far more when considering the food benefits my family was getting. $500 a month would not have given him the skills he needed to make that jump in pay. Taking another $500 a month out in taxes from others for my family and for every other eligible family would not have guaranteed there would be investments available to create and keep those $8.94-an-hour jobs. $500 a month would have made life a little easier at first, only to see it gradually eaten away by the rising costs of living and taxes but with no economic incentive or skills to get a better job and keep up.

## AN IDEA AS OLD AS TIME

Universal Basic Income (UBI) in its current variants is similar in concept to the negative income tax considered under President Nixon. The basic idea is for government to provide a guaranteed income floor for all households through a monthly check. Details, however, vary widely among the different proposals on what the income level should be, how much should be provided by the government, whether and how the assistance would be phased out as income rises, whether all persons are covered or just those affected by economic dislocation however defined, how the benefit is financed, and many other factors. All, however, share the same essential structure: cash payments sent to all adults without preconditions and for the rest of their lives with nothing expected in return.

> Offering my family $500 per month may have made us a little more comfortable in poverty, but my grandparents still would have died poor because the hurdles to get out would have been raised even higher.

Starting with the foundational texts of Western Civilization, the concept of paradise has been associated with the basics of life being provided by the governing power: And the Lord God commanded the man, saying, "You may freely eat of every tree in the garden . . ." (Genesis 2:16)

This notion continued to find its way into the literature of many periods. Thomas More's *Utopia* (1516) envisioned a society where everyone's needs were provided through centralized warehouses— including two slaves per household drawn from war captives and criminals.[8]

More's contemporary Johannes Ludovicus Vives in *On Assistance to the Poor* (1525) laid out detailed recommendations to the city government of Bruges in what is now Belgium. Vives' proposal was to provide a specified level of support to the poor to replace the more uncertain charity historically coming from the Church, but also incorporated craft training to move the poor to self-supporting employment.[9]

In a period of revolution towards the end of the 18th century, the creation of new systems of political rights also led many to consider the issues of economic rights[10] much as New Deal proponents later sought to enshrine their policies in constitutional terms. In the new United States, Thomas Paine in his

*Rights of Man* (1791-1792) laid out guaranteed payments as a matter of economic justice, explicitly rejecting any notion of means testing. As government administration was made more honest and efficient as outlined in his other writings, Paine believed existing taxes should produce a growing surplus over necessary public expenditures, which was to be used to replace the existing poor laws with guaranteed payments but only to the elderly and parents of young children. The remainder of this surplus was to be used for education, marriage allowances, and funeral benefits.

In the more radical *Agrarian Justice* (1795), Paine sought to redefine property rights as stemming only from any improvements to property or its production capacity rather than the land itself. Instead, land remained a communal resource, and landowners consequently owed a ground-rent paid through death duties for severing the community from the land. Proceeds should be used to provide a lump sum to every person upon reaching adulthood, and annual pensions to the blind, those with disabilities, and everyone over age 50. Paine believed such payments should be made as an economic right, rather than a matter of charity.[11]

Thomas Spence in *The Rights of Infants* (1797) directly attacked Paine's ideas as too conservative. Spence followed Paine in maintaining that land should be a communal resource, but that any improvements arising from labor should be considered as well. Landowners should therefore be charged an annual rent (on land but not on other assets) to be used first to cover necessary public expenses, with the remainder to be distributed annually in an equal amount per person to "compensate" for the loss of their communal rights in the land.[12]

## THE SPEENHAMLAND SYSTEM

The first organized attempt at basic income as a welfare method came after the justices of Berkshire, England adopted the Speenhamland system in 1795. Pursued first as an emergency measure at a time of rapidly rising grain prices and attendant social discord, the traditional aid to the poor was replaced with a wage supplement determined by the price of bread. Families within the system derived their income both from their own wages plus an allowance from the poor rates that varied according to a set scale ". . . so that a minimum income should be assured to the poor irrespective of their earnings."[13] Although current sources disagree on the extent of its subsequent spread, it became the prevalent system in some form in many rural areas and some industrial cities.

One of the more complete criticisms of Speenhamland is given by Karl Polanyi in *The Great Transformation* (1944, 1957, 2001). In this period, England had already developed fully functioning markets for land and capital and was set to do the same for labor—along with market-based wages—after the Act of Settlement of 1662 rules leading to "parish serfdom" were loosened in 1795. In Polanyi's view, Speenhamland simply replaced official serfdom with welfare serfdom, delaying development of a true labor market until the early 1830s following the emergence of a middle class.[14]

Moreover, Speenhamland produced an income ceiling rather than an income floor. Under the Elizabethan poor laws, the poor were required to take any job offered regardless of wage and received aid only if no job was available. Under Speenhamland, the poor received aid regardless of what they were earning, even if they had no job at all. Wages consequently could be set at any level, with any difference made up by the payers of the poor rates.

As today's UBI programs, the system at its beginnings was lauded as changing welfare for all the right reasons. In the end, it replaced feudal rural serfdom with a new economic one:

> No measure was ever more universally popular. Parents were free of the care of their children, and children were no more dependent upon parents; employers could reduce wages at will and laborers were safe from hunger whether they were busy or slack; humanitarians applauded the measure as an act of mercy even though not of justice, and the selfish gladly consoled themselves with the thought that though it was merciful at least it was not liberal; and even ratepayers were slow to realize what would happen to the rates under a system which proclaimed the "right to live" whether a man earned a living wage or not.
>
> In the long run, the result was ghastly. Although it took some time until the self-respect of the common man sank to the low point where he preferred poor relief to wages, his wages which were subsidized from public funds were bound eventually to be bottomless, and to force him upon the rates. Little by little the people of the countryside were pauperized; the adage "once on the rates, always on the rates" was a true saying. But for the protracted effects of the allowance system, it would be impossible to explain the human and social degradation of early capitalism.[15]

Speenhamland at its essence was designed with every intention of protecting the poor from the worst effects of the Industrial Revolution. In the end, it delayed by decades—for many, up until the 1870s when recognition of the trade unions gave workers greater bargaining power over their wages—their ability to share in the dramatic rise in the standard of living it produced.

In 1830, the Swing Riots spread throughout southern England by agricultural workers angered by the subsequent low wages and poor working conditions produced by this system along with reductions in the guaranteed allowance imposed as demand outgrew the resources produced from the poor rates. Adding to the unrest was a further drop in the real value of the allowance caused by a shift in the mandatory church tithe to a cash payment from its earlier form of a crop share, payable by all regardless of religious affiliation, much as progressive regulations today continue to erode the purchasing power of lower income wages. In response to the Riots, a Royal Commission into the Operation of the Poor Laws was convened, and in their 1833 report recommended a complete overhaul of the poor relief laws, as embodied in the Reform Bill of 1832 and Poor Law Amendment of 1834 that included a ban on supplementing the wages of full-time workers.[16]

Various revisionist analyses, especially those in favor of UBI concepts today, have attempted to look back eighteen decades to find fault with the methods and data used by the Royal Commission in its report, and that led to the expansion of workhouses and lower levels of welfare throughout the rest of 19th century Britain.[17] Regardless, the outcome of this social experiment has shaped much of the debate over the issue since.

Leaping over the 19th century socialists—including criticism by Karl Marx in *Das Kapital* (1867) that the guaranteed income under Speenhamland simply reflected capitalism's tendency to force the cost of labor back to zero—and the concepts and counter-concepts to replace wages altogether, basic income schemes in the first half of the 20th century arose repeatedly during periods of economic difficulties.

Bertrand Russell, in attempting to balance the promises of income security against the threats to freedom contained in both anarchism and socialism, offered basic income as a middle course for post-World War I Britain:

> . . . the plan we are advocating amounts essentially to this: that a certain small income, sufficient for necessaries, should be secured to all, whether they work or not, and that a larger income, as much larger as might be warranted by the total amount of commodities produced, should be given to those who are willing to engage in some work which the community recognizes as useful. On this basis we may build further. I do not think it is always necessary to pay more highly work which is more skilled or regarded as socially more useful, since such work is more interesting and more respected than ordinary work, and will therefore often be preferred by those who are able to do it. But we might, for instance, give an intermediate income to those who are only willing to work half the usual number of hours, and an income above that of most workers to those who choose a specially disagreeable trade.[18]

In Russell's framework, work incentives coming from such a system would be largely irrelevant as "the comparatively small number of men with an invincible horror of work—the sort of men who now become tramps—might lead a harmless existence, without any grave danger of their becoming sufficiently numerous to be a serious burden upon the more industrious."

# BASIC INCOME CROSSES THE POND

During the Great Depression, basic income become one of many ideas put on the table to tackle soaring unemployment by convincing more to leave the labor force, including children, elderly and others competing with men—generally considered then in terms of white men—for the available jobs. Social Security, while still crafted as an income supplement, was at its heart in the beginning a measure to reduce the number of elderly who had to continue working, while the components that eventually became SSI and AFDC were targeted for the same purpose for those groups as well.

The Townsend Plan championed by Francis Townsend and his 2.2 million-strong Townsend Clubs called for an old-age pension for everyone aged 60 and older of $200 a month, at a time when the average monthly wage was only about $100. While the plan claimed it could be financed by a national transaction tax of only 2 percent, this broadly popular movement—Townsend at one point submitted petitions with 10 million signatures to Congress—would have in fact cost two-thirds of the total income produced annually in the U.S. at that time.[19]

Huey Long, in the first recommendation in his "Every Man a King" plan, promised "To limit poverty by providing that every deserving family shall share in the wealth of America for not less than one third of the average wealth, thereby to possess not less than $5,000 free of debt."[20]

Building on the social credit theories developed in Britain by C.H. Douglas,[21] radio evangelist William Aberhart became premier of Alberta, Canada in 1935 after his party ran on a platform to give each citizen $25 a month, a pledge not fulfilled after entering office but resurrected twice in the 1950s through distribution of oil dividend checks as his party returned to power.

As the 20th century moved from periodic crisis to economic prosperity, further development of the basic income concept began to take two paths. In Europe, basic income was embraced in various forms by social democrat parties as they attempted to rebrand themselves away from the less savory aspects of socialism as it was being practiced in Eastern Europe and other countries. Touted more as a means to counter the "inevitable" concentration of income and wealth under capitalism, these concepts as developed in works by Dennis Milner,[22] George D.H. Cole,[23] and James Meade[24] present basic income more as a social dividend paid to the "true owners" of the economy's resources much in the same vein as promoted by Paine and Spence. This concept is also roughly embodied in the annual payments to residents from the constitutionally created Alaska Permanent Fund supported by revenues that state receives from oil and gas development.

In the U.S., the concept was further developed instead in the context of the poverty programs, first as a replacement for and subsequently as just another addition to the growing dysfunctional mix in the welfare system. George Stigler proposed using a negative income tax as a preferable alternative to minimum wage legislation.[25] This development also includes Milton Friedman's concept of a negative income tax to replace existing means-tested assistance; the 1968 initiative by

Paul Samuelson, John Kenneth Galbraith, James Tobin, Harold Watts, Robert Lampman, and 1,200 other economists for a guaranteed income but without reference to the existing public assistance programs;[26] and the large-scale testing of the concept in the social experiments that took place beginning in the late 1960s.[27]

The Reverend Dr. Martin Luther King, Jr. embraced guaranteed incomes as well to replace the failed poverty programs. Jobs to retain the worth of the individual, however, remained an important part of his plan.[28] Dr. King, however, envisioned a guarantee at a much higher level, launching the poor directly into the middle class through a level "pegged to the median income of society, not the lowest levels of income."

## AN IDEA IN OUR TIME

Charles Murray in his *In Our Hands: A Plan to Replace the Welfare State* (2006) still grounded his arguments for UBI in civil liberties terms,[29] replacing the unwieldly poverty bureaucracy with a cash grant-based system built on the work of Stigler and Friedman. The current concepts, however, draw more from Robert Theobald's *Free Men and Free Markets* (1963) and subsequent books predicting the forthcoming division of society into the gainfully employed and a growing mass of surplus labor.

Theobald's ideas quickly found their way into the political sphere, forming the basis for proposals as diverse as *The Triple Revolution*[30] resolution signed by Michael Harrington, Tom Hayden, Robert Heilbroner, Gunnar Myrdal ("with reservations"), Linus Pauling, Theobald, and others and sent to President Lyndon Johnson in 1964; Eugene McCarthy's call for a guaranteed income in his 1968 presidential campaign; Timothy Leary's proposals in his 1969-70 run for governor of California to replace taxes with a dividend produced by running the state like a business;[31] and George McGovern's "demogrant" pledge in 1972 of a $1,000 a year grant to every person (phased out by income) that was attacked even by members of his own party.[32]

Inspired by how the concept was further developed in venture capitalist Peter Barnes' book *With Liberty and Dividends for All: How to Save Our Middle Class When Jobs Don't Pay Enough* (2014), even Hillary Clinton gave serious consideration to a guaranteed income plank in her 2016 campaign, financed by current natural resources revenues such as oil and gas along with a new financial transaction tax and carbon pricing tax. After weeks of working out the details, the idea was dropped because, as she said:

> . . . we couldn't make the numbers work. To provide a meaningful dividend each year to every citizen, you'd have to raise enormous sums of money, and that would either mean a lot of new taxes or cannibalizing other important programs. We decided it was exciting but not realistic . . .[33]

In the 2020 presidential campaign, the UBI concept has taken such forms as job guarantees proposed by candidates Kirsten Gillibrand[34] and Bernie Sanders,[35] Kamala Harris' LIFT the Middle Class Act,[36] and Andrew Yang's Freedom Dividend of $12,000 a year to everyone over the age of 18, financed by giving those now on the welfare programs a choice between the cash or the programs, a new value added tax (VAT) on all goods and services, and various new taxes including a carbon tax, financial transaction tax, the elimination of favorable tax treatment for capital gains, and eliminating the Social Security cap.[37]

Rather than concrete legislative proposals, however, the UBI concept is being kept alive primarily by a growing number of "pilot" programs that hope to counter the results from prior failed experiments[38] by somehow demonstrating that a few hundred people can be made "happier" by giving them some extra cash over the course of several months. These pilots include California-based efforts in Oakland[39] by Y Combinator's Sam Altman and in Stockton[40] backed by Facebook cofounder Chris Hughes' Economic Security Project. In 2017, Hawaii legislatively declared its population is entitled to basic financial security but put off the details through a feasibility study on how to do it.[41]

Pilot programs of varying sizes have been conducted in India,[42] Kenya and Uganda,[43] Namibia,[44] and the Netherlands.[45] A few countries have shifted a portion of their welfare programs to UBI-like components, primarily Italy,[46] Brazil,[47] and other Latin American countries adopting variants of the Brazilian system. Other larger scale efforts were shut down early as a result of political and fiscal factors as in the case of the effort in Ontario, Canada,[48] disappointing early results in the case of Finland,[49] and voter rejection—at 77 percent against—in Switzerland.[50] Proposals are still in the works in Scotland[51] and there may be a national referendum in Taiwan[52] but with no concrete expectations on when or even if they will be approved.

## WHY NOW?

Basic income schemes in Europe and elsewhere continue to be grounded more in the social democrat presumed justification of social credit or social dividend, but the concept has gained new life in the U.S. as a proposed remedy to a different social problem. In direct contrast to every other such change in the past, the more dystopian views over the future of work envision the latest technological innovation - artificial intelligence - leading to a permanent division of the population into an educated class with jobs and a displaced component working minimum wage jobs and facing a life of permanent dependence.

Many of the domestic advocates for UBI in fact come from the technology world whose business models of job disruption and replacement for everyone else are crafted around bringing such a Wellsian world into being as rapidly and as profitably as possible. They not only believe in the "inevitable" income and wealth concentration under capitalism. They intend to be the ones to benefit from it.

## BUT MORE IMPORTANT, WHY NOT?

My grandmother taught me that everything that glitters is not gold. Universal Basic Income is fool's gold that does not even attempt to offer economic empowerment.

Historic proposals around this concept arose as replacements for whatever welfare system was current—and not working—at the time. Unlike the earlier incarnations including from the early beginnings through those proposed by the likes of George Stigler, Milton Friedman, and Charles Murray, UBI is no longer intended to replace the current morass of dysfunctional assistance programs and related provisions. Like the current Earned Income Tax Credit, today's UBI would simply be just another source of aid piled on top of the existing welfare and other means-tested programs and regulatory provisions.

UBI would take the unacceptably high marginal tax rates the poor and working poor already face and raise them even higher, expanding the barriers to personal economic advancement that now keep so many at these income levels. Even the more timorous step in Andrew Yang's Freedom Dividend concept that would make the choice optional—assistance from the current programs or aid from the Dividend—faced immediate criticism from UBI enthusiasts for going too far. Stockton mayor Michael Tubbs, while praising the UBI pilot underway in his city, attacked Yang's plan by saying: "I support the conversation we're having about basic income, but I don't support any proposal that would gut the social safety net."[53]

## UBI IS AN END, NOT A BEGINNING

The history of the welfare programs has for the most part emphasized work for all but those incapable of doing so because of age, physical limits, or family responsibilities. When the War on Poverty programs strayed from this course, the pressures from all sides including those who had become dependent on them came together and forced them back through the Clinton-Gingrich welfare reforms.

At the same time there has often been an undercurrent that views good paying jobs for the poor as unrealistic and, in fact, unattainable, believing instead that capitalism by its nature is destined to create a labor surplus. Many of the New Dealers looked at the jobs situation and considered the number largely fixed. They turned first to measures that paid workers to leave the labor force and reserve the jobs that were there for working age men. These policies did little more than stabilize the situation, and real solutions had to wait until productivity growth was restored, jobs once again grew, and the skill sets improved to produce the workers needed to fill them. Even Dr. King,[54] whose economic views were influenced by this type of thinking, emphasized the importance of jobs at the much higher level of guaranteed income he proposed. He understood the importance of work in creating a sense of self-reliance, personal empowerment, and even of self-worth.

UBI and its adherents instead assume—as with so many failed prognostications of the past—that the work will not be there. Jobs, or at least the jobs that pay enough, will only go to the properly educated. For the rest, the government must provide. Robert Theobald predicted this division over a half century ago in 1963. After it failed to materialize, French economist Thomas Piketty announced its imminent arrival in his 2003 work.[55] Using long term estimates, Piketty's research shows that the top 1 percent are reaching unprecedented shares of total income. Moreover, Piketty concludes that this level of higher concentration is inevitable under capitalist economies and can only be reversed through greater government taxation and regulation.

Tired of waiting for the predictions to come true, the UBI enthusiasts now seek to legislate them into being by expanding the welfare traps that have kept so many in that place.

The reality of this vision is that food will still come from food stamps. Housing will still come from vouchers and progressively smaller, climate change compliant public rentals. Healthcare for the poor will be from government providers. UBI will now fill in the rest. There are no components to build marketable skills through improved public schools or even attempts to make sense of the training program morass that has failed to come even close to its intended goals. There are no efforts to expand opportunities to prepare this part of our population for the jobs that will evolve in the future or, in keeping with a globalist mindset, even attempt to make our nation more competitive and ensure more of those jobs will be created here. UBI as a program doesn't try to make our economy and our workers more competitive. All it does is pay people so that they don't even have to try.

## UBI DOES NOT EXPAND THE BENEFITS WORKERS WANT FROM THEIR JOBS

Government revenue structures have developed through a complex of taxes, licenses, and fees built around the traditional industries referred to by some as the legacy economy. Many of the technology businesses now seeking to replace them in particular targeted ways to get around high taxes and costly regulations to secure a competitive advantage. Amazon bypassed state sales tax laws throughout much of its life and used this cost advantage to grow to where its market size now commands more pricing control than what it previously had through sales tax avoidance. Rental car sharing services bypassed local licensing and fees on established rental car companies, and ride sharing firms bypassed the onerous cost and guild-protections embodied in the taxicab system and its regulations. Home sharing did the same. Many information-based businesses use the flexibility of an intellectual property capital base to shift revenues to lower tax rate jurisdictions, while others particularly in the so-called "green" industries such as alternative energy and vehicles demanded and received tax credits and government grants to lower the effective cost of their otherwise more costly goods.

In the process, the competitive advantages gained by this tax behavior also disrupted the employer-based benefit programs in the legacy industries created in the midst and aftermath of World War II. And to replace this security and quality of that service, UBI advocates from technology instead promote a monthly stipend from the government. Benefits will not come from their jobs, gig stints or from the companies themselves, but from the government.

## UBI STILL DOES NOT PENCIL OUT

Earlier UBI proposals took great pains to demonstrate their affordability. Even Paine's somewhat fanciful notion of increasing government inefficiency was intended to yield a substantial surplus to support his notion of social compensation. Today's concentration on waste and duplication on one end of the policy spectrum, and an almost religious belief that capitalism inevitably will lead to an overconcentration of income that can be mined forever through confiscatory level taxes on the other, do not fill the expected revenue needs.

Looking at Andrew Yang's Freedom Dividend, an analysis by the UBI Center[56] pegs the annual cost of a $12,000 per adult benefit at $2.8 trillion or 14 percent of total GDP (2018). The new taxes along with the other assumed revenues contained in this proposal would leave a shortfall of $1.4 trillion and raise the projected federal deficit by another 160 percent. A separate analysis by the Tax Foundation[57] tiering off these numbers indicates that even reducing the benefit to $9,000, the proposed VAT would have to be at 22 percent rather than Yang's 10 percent level, further raising the cost of everything Americans have to buy.

These numbers are only the beginning. Like every other benefit of this type, once in place the political pressures will be there to make it as broadly available as possible to overcome political and fiscal objections. Moreover, a separate Penn-Wharton[58] analysis of a UBI similar to Yang's plan but phased in and limited to $500 would reduce GDP by 6.1 percent and government revenues by 8.0 percent over the first decade. The need for replacing jobs with government aid would increase even more.

## UBI IGNORES THE REGIONAL DIFFERENCES IN POVERTY

For most of the country, $1,000 a month is probably sufficient to provide a basic level of living on average. But in California, $1,000 per month would not even leave enough for food and clothing let alone savings, education, or other investments to enable a household to work its way to a better future. Even in California, this outcome is based on the average—in higher cost areas such as the San Francisco Bay Area, $1,000 a month per adult would be ruinous. Regional differences could be handled through regional premiums, but there is no reason why the other states should pay to help ease the cost of policies states such as California have imposed to produce these cost of living differentials.

## UBI ABSOLVES OUR DECISION MAKERS FROM HAVING TO DEAL WITH REAL PROBLEMS

UBI is the next although rather large step, in the current policy trend of enacting subsidies rather than solutions. The poor will remain poor if they do not have the proper work skills. Even if they acquire those skills, they will remain poor if the jobs to hire them and pay them a proper wage are not there. The next generations will remain poor if they continue to be shut off from the basic means of building family wealth. UBI enacts a subsidy to absolve decision makers from having to consider why those conditions exist and making the hard choices to remedy them. It provides cover like so many other policies of the recent past that raised living costs or eliminated jobs with little consideration to those who had to pay the price.

## UBI EXPECTS PEOPLE TO FAIL

We live in a time where many want to limit the course of the public—and in some instances, increasingly private as well—discourse to terms of identity politics and victimhood. People do not succeed or fail because of what they try to do; it is because of who they are. If someone fails, it's because of our system. If they do not have a good job, own a home, or earn enough, it's because our economy is changing to make them irrelevant. It's not because they weren't prepared. It's not because they didn't try hard enough. It's not because they did not consider other options. It's not because they were so wrapped up in the growing costs of housing, food, and transportation that little else mattered. Whether it's in terms of Barack Obama's "you didn't build that" admonition or Hillary Clinton's dismissal of the "deplorables," the very concept of workers outside the storied world of technology even trying to shape their economic future is regarded as a hopeless course. UBI does nothing to build expectations. It reshapes them to having just enough to get by.

## UBI RISKS HASTENING A TWO-TIER SOCIETY

The favorable economic trends that the U.S. experienced before the coronavirus pandemic carried the risk of creating a two-tier economy, where the status of each person if not the intergenerational prospects are also determined by education. UBI as now conceived would hasten this division by raising the barriers currently in place from the existing assistance programs.

Earlier proposals such as the negative income tax concept were based on the principle that government should treat everyone the same—that tax benefits given to those who pay taxes should be equally available to the lower income households who do not. It was not, as the current iterations are designed, that life for everyone should turn out the same, or at least at some government-determination of what constitutes "same" for those viewed as too uneducated if not full-on too "deplorable" to succeed on their own.

This division at its base reflects a negative view of human worth. This is a future where the educated will find challenge and self-fulfillment through their knowledge-based work. The rest are condemned to a life of drudgery and a system without hope. To suggest that a large part of our population has no value, little to contribute to society, and is incapable of learning or taking care of themselves or their families is dehumanizing.

In his writings on the new United States, the political philosopher Alexis de Tocqueville saw the primary risk to a democracy not coming from the abrupt rise of a despot or even a turn of the voters to a dictator in time of crisis. Any such dramatic shift of this nature would be short-lived as the people react to this sudden violation of their fundamental principles. De Tocqueville instead saw the fundamental threat coming from the tendency of government to slowly expand its reach. By facing society with an ever-expanding set of rules on issues of everyday life, it weakens their resolve to engage in decisions on more important matters.[59]

One of the more profound failures of the War on Poverty and its subsequent evolution was the sapping of individual enterprise through an incomprehensible body of rules. Too many within this system have necessarily devoted their energy and creativity to working the rules in order to secure access to the assistance they need, rather than developing the skills to work their way out. UBI would expand that part of the population living to the rules rather living to their potential.

## LOOKING FOR BETTER SOLUTIONS

Income inequality is a natural condition of the world; at any moment in time, someone will be doing better than you and somebody else will be doing worse. And in a free enterprise economy like the U.S., it can also be the outcome of a surge of innovation that raises the incomes of the innovators. But it also raises the overall standard of living by creating new sources of jobs and increasing the goods and services a typical income can now buy. And when those higher incomes are used to invest through capital formation and research, the economy as a whole and workers on every level can benefit from the continuing expansion of jobs and future rounds of even greater innovation.

Income inequality can become a bad thing when used to concentrate more at the top, to protect market share rather than expanding market opportunities or when those at the top spend not only to protect what they have but spend to ensure those at the bottom will never rise to challenge them.

Extreme inequality of this nature violates our sense of what it means to be an American. It undermines our fundamental basis for democracy and freedom.

The eternal answer from those on the left regardless of the true circumstances is that some people are making too much money, so we should tax a large share of it away and distribute it to everybody else. More should go to the poor, but only after government and its followers have taken their fill. At some point, government will eventually get it right.

This attitude has driven us to the point we are today-- a mass of programs that do not work and a system that seeks to condemn greater numbers to a life on merely basic income. Government has a role, but it should not be the income source of first resort.

# CHAPTER FOUR
## Getting Out of Poverty—A Moving Target

Perspective always helps to make things clear, that is why life is lived forwards but understood backwards. Looking back from where I stand today, I understand that my grandparents were never going to build any wealth. The system was rigged to keep them in a permanent state of neediness. Whether by design or accident, my grandparents had no choice but to live paycheck to paycheck just to qualify for the very public assistance that was created to help them find independence.

My grandmother stopped working so that we could report a "low enough" household income to qualify for the basic welfare programs of the day. That meant we did not have excess cashflow to save for a down payment on a real home that would have created wealth over time unlike the trailer we lived in that lost value every year. We could not save to finance a car or even pay for education. Add to these paycheck-to-paycheck qualification standards, the rising cost of living for basic needs like gas, utilities and food only compounded the pressure to "just get by". Now, it is so simple to see how my grandparents became enslaved by the anti-poverty welfare programs. That dependency did not end until my mom broke the cycle and paved the way for my sister and me.

The current divides in income and wealth are used to justify redistribution schemes and confiscatory level tax increases in the name of helping people in poverty. And these ideas are promoted without consideration to the overall effects on the incentives to achieve and excel within the U.S. economic system, the ability to continue the cycles of innovation that have boosted economic well-being, and the general urge to do better, prepare one's children for a bright future, and avoid falling into the stasis of government dependency.

Most Americans do not want to be fed and housed by Bill Gates, Warren Buffett, and Elon Musk. They want to *be* Bill Gates, Warren Buffett, or Elon Musk, or at least given the opportunity through a career or as an entrepreneur to make a decent living, own a home, educate their children, and ensure a decent retirement. Wages and incomes have improved, but not at the pace needed to broaden the population capable of reaching these goals.

Those on the extreme left make the entire issue about wages and higher taxes using imperfect data that masks the wage growth and rise in living standards that has occurred in the U.S. They limit the debate instead to the minimum wage and income redistribution. Everything will be okay, they argue, if we just raise everybody to a "living wage" level—however that is defined—or subsidize them through means such as universal basic income.

They want to reduce the debate to everyone as minimum wage slaves.

These advocates reduce wage and income issues to a few emotional and sound bite solutions. But those who live in the real world understand the costs and real-life impacts of these proposals.

If government artificially raises the cost of labor or imposes new or higher taxes on business, it raises the cost of producing goods and services. This, in turn, raises the prices paid by consumers. These may be absorbable if you live on the Westsides of Manhattan or Los Angeles and do your weekly shopping at Whole Foods. But for the working poor and other lower and even middle income groups who are aware of every price change and must stay within a monthly budget, such policies strike two ways. Raising wages help—if the jobs and hours will still be there. Rising costs hurt and can erase any real income gains.

Recent surveys[60] have asked whether the minimum wage helped the working poor. Nearly two-thirds (66 percent) somewhat or strongly agreed with the statement that, "a higher minimum wage helps workers like me." But a higher number—75 percent—also said that, "a higher minimum wage causes businesses to raise prices" and 66 percent agreed with the premise that, "a higher minimum wage causes landlords to raise rents."

The working poor are far more aware of the effect of supply and demand on prices than many policy gurus on the left. They have to be. My grandmothers could quote you to the penny every price for everything they had to buy each month. They knew how prices were changing, and more often than not what was causing them to change. They had to know where every cent in the household was coming from and where it had to go. They had no other choice.

In the California research of working poor taken before the COVID-19 crisis,[61] these regular folks showed a high degree of awareness of the personal options open to them for wage and income advancement, whether through training, education, opening their own business, or pursuing a better job, preferably one with benefits. But they were also concerned about potentially making the wrong job or advancement choice. If it turned out wrong, they feared that the rising costs of living would overtake them, put them further behind, or put them in a position from which it would be hard to escape. Concerns over risk kept many right where they were, making enough to get by but not enough to get ahead.

The single largest factor cited as a barrier to getting ahead is not how much the poor were earning or whether higher paid jobs were available but the high cost of living. In the survey, 88 percent cited it as a moderate or extreme barrier, while 56 percent—the only response in the double digits—cited living costs as the greatest challenge they face.

## FIGURE 2. SURVEY OF WORKING POOR: COSTS OF LIVING

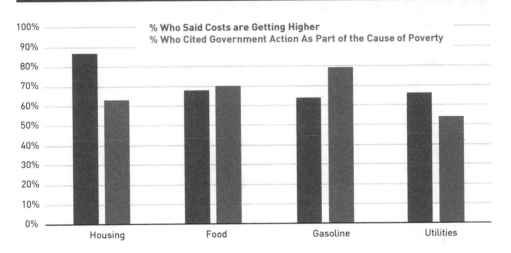

*Source: Vision Strategy and Insights, Barriers to Economic Development in California Quantitative Research Report, November 2017*

As shown in Figure 2, sizeable portions of the working poor were also aware of how specific government actions were part of the cause. They understand that it was government policy behind the lack of housing supply, causing housing costs to grow. They knew that increasing minimum wage and labor costs resulted in higher food costs. California's formulation regulations led to higher gasoline prices, and the state's climate change regulations led to the rising costs for electricity. Each regulation was enacted with good intent but ignored how higher costs would hurt the working poor the most. In bad news for proponents of big government mandates, these working poor showed a high degree of awareness of who has been left on the hook.

## FIGURE 3. TOP 25 CITIES BY NONFARM JOBS CHANGE, SUPPLEMENTAL POVERTY MEASURE THRESHOLD RANK

| | Change in Jobs, 2007 – 2018 (1,000) | Jobs Change Rank | SPM 2018 Threshold | SPM Threshold Rank |
|---|---|---|---|---|
| San Jose-Sunnyvale-Santa Clara, CA | 199.7 | 17 | $39,607 | 1 |
| San Francisco-Oakland-Hayward, CA | 373.0 | 5 | $37,052 | 2 |
| Washington-Arlington-Alexandria, DC-VA-MD-WV | 294.3 | 8 | $35,513 | 5 |
| Los Angeles-Long Beach-Anaheim, CA | 380.5 | 4 | $34,308 | 7 |
| San Diego-Carlsbad, CA | 162.3 | 22 | $33,829 | 10 |
| Boston-Cambridge-Nashua, MA-NH | 287.4 | 10 | $33,146 | 12 |
| New York-Newark-Jersey City, NY-NJ-PA | 962.9 | 1 | $32,943 | 13 |
| Seattle-Tacoma-Bellevue, WA | 288.5 | 9 | $30,809 | 21 |
| Miami-Fort Lauderdale-West Palm Beach, FL | 257.6 | 12 | $30,736 | 23 |
| Austin-Round Rock, TX | 297.0 | 7 | $29,952 | 28 |
| Denver-Aurora-Lakewood, CO | 259.6 | 11 | $29,836 | 29 |
| Philadelphia-Camden-Wilmington, PA-NJ-DE-MD | 129.3 | 25 | $29,314 | 35 |
| Riverside-San Bernardino-Ontario, CA | 213.9 | 14 | $29,038 | 37 |
| Minneapolis-St. Paul-Bloomington, MN-WI | 164.2 | 21 | $28,413 | 46 |
| Chicago-Naperville-Elgin, IL-IN-WI | 189.3 | 19 | $28,297 | 49 |
| Orlando-Kissimmee-Sanford, FL | 211.2 | 16 | $28,123 | 52 |
| Portland-Vancouver-Hillsboro, OR-WA | 152.0 | 23 | $28,021 | 54 |
| Dallas-Fort Worth-Arlington, TX | 679.5 | 2 | $27,673 | 59 |
| Atlanta-Sandy Springs-Roswell, GA | 325.7 | 6 | $27,339 | 67 |
| Houston-The Woodlands-Sugar Land, TX | 498.5 | 3 | $27,237 | 71 |
| Phoenix-Mesa-Scottsdale, AZ | 189.3 | 18 | $26,947 | 82 |
| San Antonio-New Braunfels, TX | 212.1 | 15 | $26,831 | 86 |
| Nashville-Davidson-Murfreesboro-Franklin, TN | 217.4 | 13 | $26,294 | 107 |
| Columbus, OH | 138.7 | 24 | $25,974 | 115 |
| Charlotte-Concord-Gastonia, NC-SC | 183.0 | 20 | $25,713 | 129 |

*Source: Metropolitan Statistical Areas or MSAs , U.S. Bureau of Labor Statistics; U.S. Census Bureau*

The importance of costs to income levels can be illustrated through an exercise using the 2018 Supplemental Poverty Measure (SPM) from the U.S. Census Bureau.[62] It is a more precise measure of poverty that takes into account more sources of (noncash) government assistance, along with regional differences in the cost of living represented by the cost of housing (which includes housing itself, utilities, taxes, and property insurance). Going to the top 25 MSAs that account for 66 percent of the net job growth between 2007 and 2018, Figure 3 shows their rank according to the 2018 poverty threshold for a two adult/two child family of renters.

Figure 3 provides two insights. First, it is entirely possible to have significant job growth without government actions that jack up the cost of living for workers who need to live in these areas in order to get those jobs. Five of these top MSAs by jobs fall within the second quartile when ranked by SPM threshold.

Second, the difference between the highest and lowest cost-adjusted poverty thresholds in this figure is $13,894, or the equivalent of $6.68 an hour. This is 34 percent higher than California's $5 an hour increase to its minimum wage enacted in 2016, or 55 percent or higher if the average number of hours worked is taken into account.

In other words, actions that *remove* or reduce government involvement—reforms to zoning and land use provisions that restrict construction of new housing and the many regulations, fees, taxes, and regulatory/litigation delays that pump up the cost of what little is built in many coastal urban centers—would do far more to alleviate poverty conditions than government control of wages. Instead of using government mandates to subsidize the cost effects of these policies on the working poor—and many middle income and higher as well—a shift to market-based solutions to increase housing supply and reduce housing costs would provide greater income relief in these areas, allow these workers to move closer to where the jobs are being created, and reduce the need for longer commutes. It would also allow more time to be spent with their families or upgrading their skills and longer-term income prospects.

> A rise in income means nothing if it is overwhelmed by a significant rise in the basic costs of household life.

Advocates for government control of wages and redistribution of income also push for increased regulations that would affect costs for housing, food, transportation, taxes, and other necessities of life. A rise in income means nothing if it is overwhelmed by a significant rise in the basic costs of household life. Being on the edge, the working poor are keenly aware of this balance. Policymakers should take note, as well.

A key finding from the California Business Roundtable research[63] is that the working poor are well aware of their options to pursue higher wages with their employers and what they had to do to qualify for better paying and higher benefit jobs. What held many back however, was that the target is always moving. Costs for the basic necessities are constantly rising, eating up whatever progress they were able to make in wage growth. Even worse, the need to keep up with basic living costs has made them risk averse, eroding whatever margin of financial safety they had and raising the consequences—a return to complete government dependence—of choosing the wrong training program, job change, or concept from which to start their own business. Their view was not so much that their wages were not rising enough, but more that costs overshadowed whatever progress they were able to make.

This risk aversion is a consequence of the current "progressive" model.

Current policies towards the poor and the working poor trace their roots to the Progressive era—from the New Deal, to the Fair Deal, to the Great Society. But the Progressive era has now morphed into a new "progressive" model that fundamentally sees an end to economic growth for a substantial slice of society. The participating part is now left out or at best reserved for the properly credentialed few, and benefitting is increasingly described only in terms of redistribution.

The policies promoted by several 2020 Democratic presidential candidates and adopted in so-called progressive states encompass an increasingly incompatible set of goals. On one hand is the demand for good paying jobs for the traditional base of the poor, working poor, and working middle class who provide the votes. On the other is the social, environmental, and globalist agendas of the elites who fund the campaigns.

The end result of this policy tension is not hard to envision, for it is already playing out in the states that have fully embraced the "progressive" model.

# CHAPTER FIVE

## Case Study: California
## How Progressive Policies Increase Costs of Living and Keep People in Poverty

They say that so goes California, so goes the nation.

As we have seen many times over the years with political movements, this is definitely true. Unfortunately, this can be both good and bad. The recent policy trends from my home state, which embrace the progressive model of high taxes, costly regulations, and more government control over our daily lives, are not beneficial at all for poor Californians.

In fact, the policies embraced by state policymakers make life much more expensive and difficult for working class Californians and those trying to escape poverty and move up the economic ladder. The big government agenda emanating from Sacramento is very regressive, contributing to the state's status as first in the nation for poverty.

This political agenda of high taxes, high fees, and high regulation is now being exported throughout the country to states in the Pacific Northwest, Hawaii, and New York.

Below are a few examples of how well-intentioned big government policies are increasing costs of living for millions and keeping more people trapped in poverty.

# HOUSING

Housing costs continue to rise for the simple fact that high costs embodied in California's regulatory, permit, and fiscal policies have worked against building more houses. Based on permit data from the state Department of Finance and California Construction Industry Research Board, there have only been three years since 1990 when new housing has come even close to or met the level required just to keep up with that year's population growth. None has been built to tackle the growing supply deficit. This point was even acknowledged in Governor Gavin Newsom's campaign promises to enact reforms to produce the 3.5 million new units by 2025 required to alleviate the housing shortage and bring costs back under control.

As a result, while owning your own home was part of the original California Dream promising and for many decades delivering on a middle class life, home ownership and its role in generational wealth acquisition has become an option reserved increasingly for only those with higher incomes in the new progressive period. As shown in Figure 4, the latest American Community Survey data show home ownership rates are lower in California across the income spectrum, but gaps are the strongest in the lower- and middle-income ranges. In the progressive model, investing in the future increasingly has become a luxury good.

**FIGURE 4. HOME OWNERSHIP BY HOUSEHOLD INCOME: CALIFORNIA VS. REST OF U.S.**

*Source: American Community Survey, 2018*

As California continues to turn its back on its Dream and shifts closer to becoming a state of renters, rents are high and getting higher as shown in Figure 5. The highest rents are generally in the coastal urban areas where the higher paying jobs are, while lower rents are generally in the interior regions with fewer good-paying job opportunities. This presents the working poor, and increasingly the middle-income households, with a trade-off between finding housing they can afford and long and expensive commutes—both in time and actual expenses—to get to where the jobs are.

Overcrowding, defined as more than one person living in a household per room, also has become an option for many, with the American Community Survey data pegging California's overcrowding rate in renter-occupied units at 13 percent in 2018, compared to the rest of the U.S. at only 5 percent.

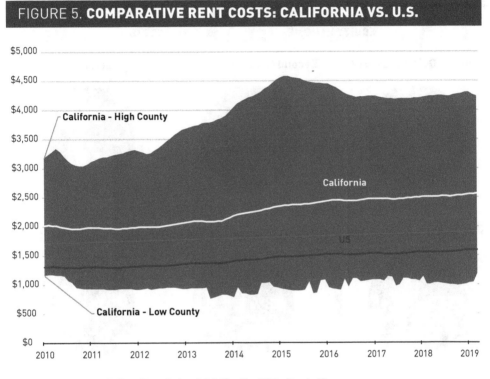

## FIGURE 5. COMPARATIVE RENT COSTS: CALIFORNIA VS. U.S.

*Source: Zillow Data, Zillow Rent Index, Multifamily, SFC, Condo/Coop*

The progressive model response has been to discuss the problem as one of affordable housing. Rather than easing the high permit, regulatory, and fee costs that make it economically infeasible to build new homes and has put homeownership out of range for more Californians each year, the primary policy responses have focused on subsidies for affordable housing, both directly through funding and indirectly by inclusionary policies that raise the cost of market-rate housing even higher. While talking about the need to make homebuilding economical out of one side of their mouths, elected officials too often protect the regulations and policies that are causing the state's home affordability problem in the first place, beginning with the California Environmental Quality Act.

For most Americans the primary paths to wealth acquisition and security fall within three options: (1) buying a primary home to live in and then a second to rent out, (2) starting and growing a business, and (3) investing in employer-based retirement plans, their own IRA/401(k)s and Social Security and Medicare. Outside of the accrual value of their Social Security and Medicare benefits, owning a home remains the primary source for most income levels. As shown in Figure 6, home equity comprises over half of the net worth for the bottom 80 percent of households by income, and roughly two-thirds for the bottom 60 percent.

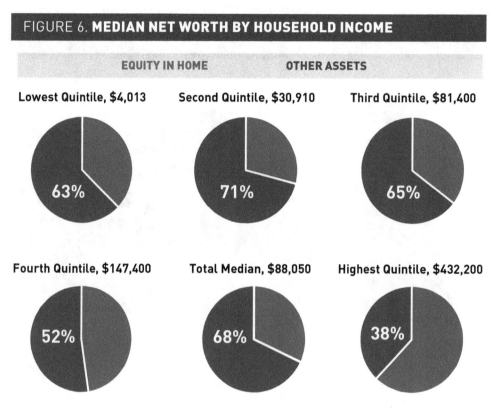

FIGURE 6. **MEDIAN NET WORTH BY HOUSEHOLD INCOME**

EQUITY IN HOME          OTHER ASSETS

Lowest Quintile, $4,013    Second Quintile, $30,910    Third Quintile, $81,400

63%    71%    65%

Fourth Quintile, $147,400    Total Median, $88,050    Highest Quintile, $432,200

52%    68%    38%

*Source: U.S. Census Bureau, Wealth and Asset Ownership, 2015*

Ownership rates, however, have generally declined in the period after 2007, with all income groups falling below their prior peak share, and about half the income groups (20-39.9 percent, 40-59.9 percent, and Top 10 percent) below their 1989 levels.[64] The greatest drops from the peak have been in the lower three income groups (drop of 5.8 to 7.8 percentage points) with smaller gaps (drop of 3.2 to 4.9 percentage points) remaining for the top three.

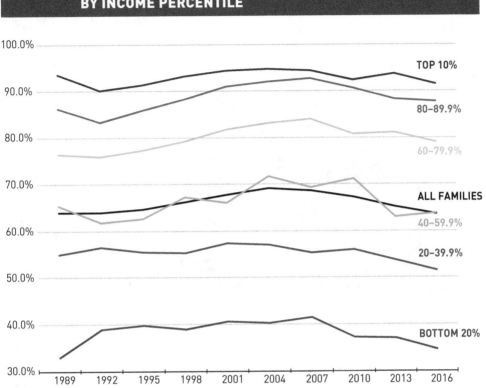

**FIGURE 7. SHARE OF FAMILIES OWNING A PRIMARY RESIDENCE BY INCOME PERCENTILE**

*Source: Federal Reserve System, Survey of Consumer Finances, Internal Data Series*

Housing ownership was rising in the period prior to the 2008 recession, in part because new housing supply was being built at much faster rates and in a broader range of offerings including options that were more affordable to the bottom 60 percent. As shown in Figure 7, new housing starts peaked in 2005, but then fell to just above a quarter of this previous high in 2009 and 2010. Housing prices also fell during this period, but fewer were able to buy. Jobs and income fell even more severely as a result of the Dodd-Frank Act in 2010, reducing credit availability to lower and middle-income households.

FIGURE 8. **HOUSING STARTS BY REGION**

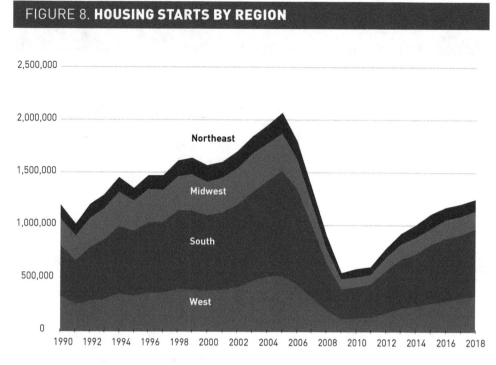

Source: U.S. Census Bureau

Housing starts have since risen, but only to the level of the 1990s recessionary years and not yet to the scale necessary to address backlogged demand, let alone produce the additional supply required to bring prices back to an affordable level. This is particularly true in coastal urban areas that had led an undue portion of job growth prior to the coronavirus-fueled economic downturn. The consequences of this situation to wealth inequality are explored in Figure 9.

Looking again at the top 25 MSAs ranked by net job growth, Figure 9 also estimates the income required to afford the median value home in 2018. The incomes are estimated by: (1) using the median home value in each MSA from the Zillow Home Value Index (ZHVI);[65] (2) calculating the required mortgage payment assuming 10 percent down and the average 2018, 30-year fixed rate mortgage, and (3) calculating the required qualifying income based on mortgage payments being no more than 25 percent of income. Note that these calculations account only for the mortgage payments, and do not include the other cost components of property tax, insurance, and monthly utilities that are typically included in housing affordability measures.

Using average earnings by educational attainment from Figure 21, a household with only one wage earner—a typical one parent with children situation—with a high school diploma or less would be unable to qualify for the median value home in any of the MSAs where the most jobs have been created. A household with two earners at less than a high school wage level would qualify in 12 of the MSAs on paper, but only if the wages of one were not being eaten by childcare costs that would put them out of the game.

These numbers are of course medians, and housing is also available at price points below the median. But in recent years and especially in the hottest job markets, this housing has instead been snapped up by higher incomes otherwise shut out of the bidding for homes at the higher points they once thought they could afford.

FIGURE 9. **TOP 25 MSAS BY NONFARM JOBS CHANGE, 2018 INCOME REQUIRED FOR MEDIAN VALUE HOME**

| | Change in Jobs, 2007 - 2018 (1,000) | Jobs Change Rank | Required Income |
|---|---|---|---|
| San Jose-Sunnyvale-Santa Clara, CA | 199.7 | 17 | $237,603 |
| San Francisco-Oakland-Hayward, CA | 373.0 | 5 | $168,837 |
| Los Angeles-Long Beach-Anaheim, CA | 380.5 | 4 | $135,001 |
| San Diego-Carlsbad, CA | 162.3 | 22 | $121,553 |
| Seattle-Tacoma-Bellevue, WA | 288.5 | 9 | $97,146 |
| Boston-Cambridge-Nashua, MA-NH | 287.4 | 10 | $92,812 |
| Denver-Aurora-Lakewood, CO | 259.6 | 11 | $85,476 |
| New York-Newark-Jersey City, NY-NJ-PA | 962.9 | 1 | $84,287 |
| Portland-Vancouver-Hillsboro, OR-WA | 152.0 | 23 | $83,079 |
| Washington-Arlington-Alexandria, DC-VA-MD-WV | 294.3 | 8 | $82,775 |
| Riverside-San Bernardino-Ontario, CA | 213.9 | 14 | $76,188 |
| Austin-Round Rock, TX | 297.0 | 7 | $64,305 |
| Miami-Fort Lauderdale-West Palm Beach, FL | 257.6 | 12 | $56,013 |
| Dallas-Fort Worth-Arlington, TX | 679.5 | 2 | $55,947 |
| Minneapolis-St. Paul-Bloomington, MN-WI | 164.2 | 21 | $54,812 |
| Nashville-Davidson-Murfreesboro-Franklin, TN | 217.4 | 13 | $54,275 |
| Orlando-Kissimmee-Sanford, FL | 211.2 | 16 | $51,702 |
| Phoenix-Mesa-Scottsdale, AZ | 189.3 | 18 | $51,134 |
| Chicago-Naperville-Elgin, IL-IN-WI | 189.3 | 19 | $48,524 |
| Charlotte-Concord-Gastonia, NC-SC | 183.0 | 20 | $47,077 |
| Atlanta-Sandy Springs-Roswell, GA | 325.7 | 6 | $45,222 |
| Philadelphia-Camden-Wilmington, PA-NJ-DE-MD | 129.3 | 25 | $43,910 |
| Tampa-St. Petersburg-Clearwater, FL | 121.1 | 26 | $42,586 |
| Houston-The Woodlands-Sugar Land, TX (Harris Co. ZHVI) | 498.5 | 3 | $40,360 |
| Columbus, OH | 138.7 | 24 | $40,012 |
| San Antonio-New Braunfels, TX (Bexar Co. ZHVI) | 212.1 | 15 | $38,456 |

*Source: U.S. Bureau of Labor Statistics; Zillow Data, ZHVI All Homes*

The effective results from the policy responses to the 2008 housing crash largely consisted of taking the working poor and middle-class levels and turning many of them from being homeowners into a perpetual renter class. Policy decisions focused on "rescuing" homeowners from underwater mortgages—along with the Wall Street firms holding those mortgages—rather than seeking ways to keep families in their homes through mortgage refinancing, debt relief, or bringing the 6.3 percent average mortgage rate in 2007 down more quickly to the 3.7 percent it reached in 2012.[66] Policymakers also ignored the tried-and-true recessionary responses of tax and regulatory relief.

The tenor at that time was that the housing market was down, and the "failures of capitalism" meant markets could only go down with little recognition that the nation had gone through similar cycles repeatedly in the past. Investors, both foreign and domestic, began snatching up properties as the owners were stampeded into walking away. As an opportunity not to be wasted, the circumstances were used instead to extend government regulation of financial and credit markets, expand regulation of housing, and turn the purpose of housing for many from a wealth building opportunity to yet another area of life that should instead be provided through government.

The policy focus, especially in those states and urban areas with the worst housing shortages such as in California, continues to treat these income groups as renters. Answers for the poor and the working poor are limited to housing vouchers and the construction of more affordable housing, including through inclusionary provisions that require such housing to be a set-aside in any new housing development and thereby shift the cost of this mandate from government to market rate housing and pushing the prices beyond reach for many even more.

> As more households in lower and middle-income ranges become renters, this is the way of life that will be taught to their children.

The housing policies embodied in many state and city climate change policies—and enforced through plans, zoning, and environmental review-related litigation—concentrate this policy focus even more by encouraging housing to be higher density, multi-unit buildings, preferably built in a transit-dependent setting. What these requirements mean in practice is that new housing will become smaller, more expensive, and affordable to lower incomes only if subsidized and rented rather than owned.[67] Lower income workers especially those with larger households instead will be forced into longer commutes as they seek suitable housing they can afford, shifting the time they could be spending with family and developing skills instead to being stuck in traffic congestion and waiting in yet another line.

Beyond the actual effect on generational mobility options is the diminishment this current situation threatens to impose on those even considering mobility as a choice. As more households in lower and middle-income ranges become renters, this is the way of life that will be taught to their children. While their peers in the higher income levels go on to build wealth through buying their own homes and inheriting property from their parents, a growing renter class runs the risk of becoming divorced from even the concept of home ownership as an option, a risk that will become all too real as state and local policies push to enforce it. And in an era of hyper-low interest rates when little Johnny and Suzie realize they can only get a dollar or two a year from saving instead of spending their allowances and birthday cash, the very concept of saving and investing for the future becomes increasingly abstract and missing in their daily experiences.

## ENERGY COSTS

Adding to California's increased cost of living are expensive energy burdens driven by state government's climate change policies. As shown in Figure 10, the average residential electric bill has increased 24 percent since 2010 when these policies began while the monthly bills have largely remained level in the rest of the country. These numbers, however, are state averages. From California Energy Commission data, average household electricity use in 2018 was as much as 69 percent higher in the hotter and colder interior regions, compared to the milder climate coastal areas. In other words, the lower income and increasingly middle-income workers forced to live in those interior regions also must bear a far greater share of the cost coming from the state's progressive energy policies. Their jobs and the wages those jobs can pay are also being affected, with the same data (12-month moving averages) showing commercial electricity rates in California are now 65 percent above the average for the rest of the U.S. and industrial rates 104 percent higher.

As the Pacific Research Institute has documented, "Currently, California implements 218 different energy efficiency regulations, incentives, and tax programs that reduce job and income growth across the state but are felt more severely in the Central Valley and Inland Empire regions, which are not fully benefiting from the prosperity along the coast."[68]

California's big government energy agenda particularly impacts poor, rural, minority, and inland communities. Monthly power bills, for example, are 57 percent higher on average during the summer months than in coastal communities.[69] As unemployment rates are higher in the Inland Empire and Central Valley, residents in these communities can't afford these higher energy costs.

And these costs have come with little practical effect. U.S. Environmental Protection Agency data[70] shows the U.S. as a whole by 2017 reduced its global warming emissions to only 1.3 percent above the 1990 level, while California[71] was 1.6 percent below that year. Comparing the year-to-year numbers, the U.S. as a whole, by largely using more market-oriented measures, is only running 1-2 years behind California's far more costly regulatory mandates favored by the progressive model.

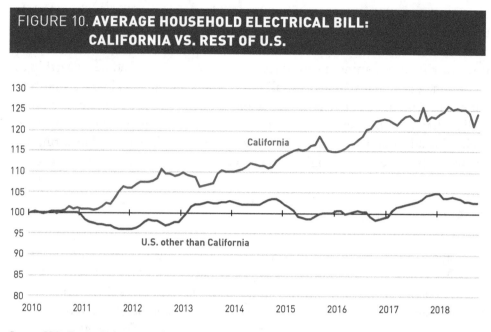

**FIGURE 10. AVERAGE HOUSEHOLD ELECTRICAL BILL: CALIFORNIA VS. REST OF U.S.**

*Source: U.S. Energy Information Administration, 12 month running average; 2010=100*

## FOOD

Measures such as minimum wage hikes and tax increases can have some positive effects on the working poor if the resulting income and public services directly benefit them. As is typically the case, these measures also bring more harm than good as the increased costs they trigger on manufacturers and services providers are passed on to consumers through higher prices.

One area where this effect is notably taking place is in food costs. Figure 11 shows the relative price change (prior to the coronavirus) for food consumption at home (groceries prepared at home) compared to food consumed away from home (restaurant and take-out food) using a formula developed by the state Department of Finance to construct a California CPI from the indices published by U.S. Bureau of Labor Statistics. California, like much of the U.S. in recent years has even seen deflationary trends for food at home. As commutes have grown longer due to the housing situation, purchasing food away from home has grown in significance for low- and middle-income households. Combining rising state energy, rents, and labor costs triggered by state mandates such as a $15 state minimum wage by 2022, California consumers have seen prices for this increasingly important component of the food budget rise by more than 40 percent.

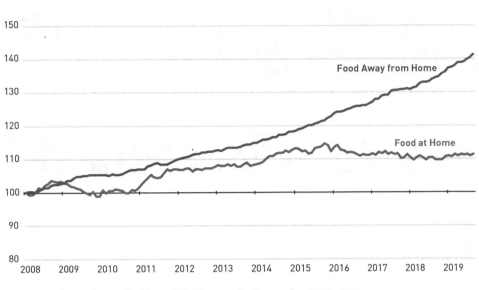

**FIGURE 11. CALIFORNIA FOOD COSTS**

Food Away from Home

Food at Home

*Source: California Center for Jobs and the Economy, Indicators; Jan 2008=100*

## TRANSPORTATION

California's substantially higher transportation costs are the result of three components. First is direct regulation. Fuels sold within the state must comply with specific formulations adopted under clean air regulations plus additional provisions adopted under the state's climate change program including additional formulation requirements, and the cost of emission credits for both production and subsequent consumer use of the fuels. Second, California in 2017 increased fuel taxes to what are now the highest levels in the nation.

Third, compliant fuel is more expensive to produce, and noncompliant fuel cannot be sold within the state. As a result, California's fuel market has been walled off from the rest of the nation and world since the first provisions were imposed in the early 1990s. Even as U.S. standards have closed over the years with California's, the state has continued to maintain this regulatory wall by upping the requirements even further. As a result, few and in some years no alternative supplies are available during spot shortages brought on with some regularity as a result of accidents or delays during the biannual refinery changeover between the summer and winter formulation rules. This factor produces considerable price volatility in different regions of the state.

The combination of these factors has seen fuel prices (prior to the significant drop in fuel demand due to coronavirus-related shelter-in-place orders and the unrelated global oil price war) average 38 percent higher than the rest of the U.S. in the period shown in Figure 8, spiking to as much as 64 percent higher.

Progressives argue that these are justifiable and absorbable costs because their goal is to force consumer changes to adapt to climate change. As shortages and price spikes—yet again—appear due to the latest mishap at the refineries, the first response of the political hierarchy has been to say nothing, hoping to weather the latest event with their climate change regulations intact. When price spikes persist, they typically pass the buck by calling for an official investigation to try and change the subject, when they know government policies are the primary culprit for rising fuel prices.

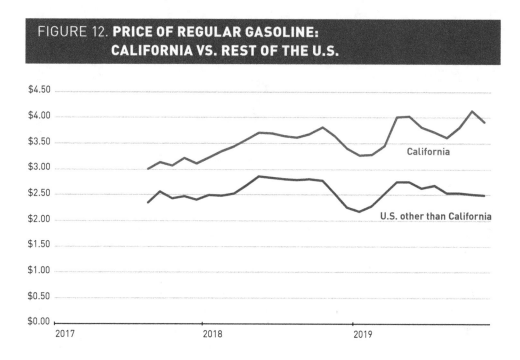

FIGURE 12. **PRICE OF REGULAR GASOLINE: CALIFORNIA VS. REST OF THE U.S.**

*Source: GasBuddy as contained in Center for Jobs & the Economy, Indicators*

The broader response has been to shift spending priorities from the roads that workers, businesses, and the general public actually use to public transit that each year fewer and fewer use. Public transit (all forms) ridership measured in UPT (unlinked passenger trips) has fallen over the past three years, to below the 2002 level in California's case in spite of the billions spent to expand the state's systems.

Other government policies on transportation involve government playing car salesman, offering taxpayer-funded subsidies to encourage motorists to buy zero emission vehicles (ZEVs), or electric-powered cars. But these subsidies are not benefitting poor and middle-class drivers who can't afford the expensive price tags of these cars, which often exceed $40,000. They only benefit the wealthy. As found in the Pacific Research Institute study *Costly Subsidies for the Rich*, 79 percent of electric vehicle plug-in tax credits were claimed by households with adjusted gross incomes of greater than $100,000 per year.[72]

These results are not surprising. Most public transit systems, especially the more convenient rail systems, are set up to serve areas with significant centers concentrating higher wage professional and technical jobs such as in New York City, Boston, San Francisco, and Silicon Valley. Lower- and increasingly middle-income workers, as they are pushed out by housing costs, instead rely on personal vehicles to reach a larger, more diversified selection of job opportunities. They have to diversify their options to stabilize their incomes. Even in New York City, the most transit dense region in the country, a typical worker has access to six times as many jobs traveling 30 minutes by car than they do by using public transit.[73]

As the Pacific Research Institute found, if California repealed its mandates that are primarily responsible for the spikes in gasoline prices, "state consumers could save between $9.5 billion and $9.6 billion annually, depending upon the assumptions regarding how many of the total miles driven in 2019 were due to electric vehicles."[74]

FIGURE 13. **PUBLIC TRANSIT RIDERSHIP (UPT)**

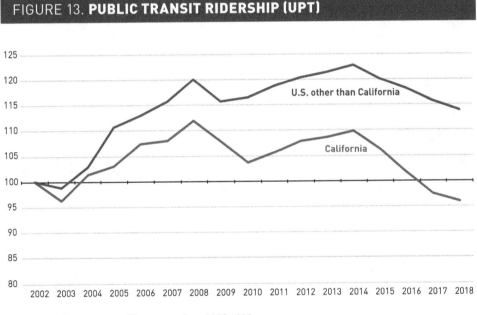

*Source: U.S. Department of Transportation; 2002=100*

# THE PROGRESSIVE PENALTY

The consequences of the high cost of living associated with the current progressive model is that, in the high job growth areas such as Silicon Valley and the broader Bay Area, even households earning six figures find it difficult to make ends meet. For the poor, the outcome is even more pressing.

To illustrate, Figure 14 compares just two core costs of living—housing and transportation—for a household with earned income of $25,000 for California, Los Angeles County, and the U.S.

## FIGURE 14. AVERAGE COSTS OF LIVING

|  | California | Los Angeles | Rest of U.S. |
|---|---|---|---|
| Wages | $25,000 | $25,000 | $25,000 |
| FICA | $3,800 | $3,800 | $3,800 |
| Rent | 14,170 | 15,610 | 8,690 |
| Electricity | 1,040 | 850 | 1,280 |
| Gas | 340 | 330 | 340 |
| Water | 710 | 580 | 550 |
| Fuel | 1,600 | 1,630 | 1,220 |
| Fuel Tax | 420 | 420 | 280 |
| Vehicle Insurance | 3,280 | 4,010 | 2,570 |
| Total Selected Expenses | $25,360 | $27,230 | $18,730 |
| Net Income | -$360 | -$2,230 | $6,270 |

Source: California Center for Jobs & the Economy

Note: The numbers in general—which are from before the COVID-19 crisis—were developed as follows:[75] 1) Rent and water costs are from an analysis of the American Community Survey, public use microdata (through ipums.org) of rent paid by households earning $0 to $50,000. Electricity and natural gas costs are from the same source, adjusted to conform to the actual usage levels and rates reported by the U.S. Energy Information Administration. 2) Fuel costs are based on mileage for renters from the 2017 National Household Travel Survey, two vehicles per household with the second driven half as much as the first, average fuel efficiency from U.S. Department of Transportation, and average fuel costs from GasBuddy.com. Fuel taxes are from American Petroleum Institute. Insurance costs are from Zebra State of Auto Insurance Reports.

The cost of living penalty stemming from the progressive model from just these two expense categories totals $6,630 on average for the state as a whole, and $8,500 for those living in Los Angeles County. In both cases, average costs alone more than cover earned income, forcing this hypothetical household into choices such as doubling up with other family members or friends, balancing the trade-off between lower rent and higher commuting, or driven into dependence on government aid simply by these two costs of living.

The typical response of the progressive model is to ignore the source of these costs entirely. Fixing the problem would entail reforming or even eliminating regulations that others within their coalition, generally with higher incomes, hold dear.

Instead, the first response from the progressive model is to conclude that the poor "can't afford to live" on what they're being given and use these conditions to push for higher assistance levels. When that fails, they then push to increase regulations even more, through rent control, restrictions on driving, rules to force people out of their cars, and others that make the supply and cost conditions even worse. And when more regulations fail to fix the problem, they propose a government take-over of that part of the economy under the assumption that this time, the government will figure out how to run it better and provide the services at a level that people will actually want.

Dealing effectively with poverty should mean stop moving the goal.

# CHAPTER SIX
## The Hollowing Out of Middle-Class Jobs and What that Means for the Working Poor

I grew up in a poor rural town in an unincorporated area of Mansfield, Texas. The only middle-class jobs available required a college degree, and nobody in my family had a college degree. Those jobs were limited to government, education, and public safety and there were too few spots to raise the economic floor of the entire community. The successful and growing companies would invest in metro areas where there was an abundance of skilled labor. The only people moving into Mansfield at the time were poor people seeking a lower cost of living to get by on their welfare payments. With little to no upward economic opportunity, our area just went through a vicious cycle of lower income people moving in and second and third generations of poor families settling for a quality of life chained to welfare programs. Those of us who found a way out, never went back, not because we did not want to... there simply was no opportunity there to pursue. The poor settled and the educated left.

The U.S. began as a largely rural country with an agrarian economy. Some of our early leaders including Thomas Jefferson believed we should stay that way, forming a nation of citizen farmers much in the way of a romanticized notion of the Roman Republic. As industrialization and agricultural mechanization pulled millions from the farms to the cities, Marx and the other socialist theorists instead saw the end of capitalism through the immiseration of workers and the seeds of revolution.

In the U.S., by the 1800s, three-quarters of the U.S. population worked on farms falling to only one-fifth by the 1930s and 8 percent by 1960. Manufacturing went from 32 percent of U.S. jobs in 1920 to 9 percent in 2015. Domestic services went from 9 percent in 1920 to essentially negligible today. Services (other than finance, trade, transportation, and government) went from 13 percent in 1900 to 34 percent in 2018.[76] In each of these cycles and the cycles within them, the economy consistently created more jobs than it had before. Jobs became more varied, more available, and the real incomes of workers grew while what they could afford to buy grew as well.

Jobs have been reinvented from old concepts: boarding houses became Airbnb; renting out your wagon services outside the growing season became Uber and Lyft; milkmen and delivery boys from the local store turned into Amazon; matchmakers into Craig's List and less savory sites; and party line telephones into Facebook.

> In the Post-Industrial era, services and knowledge-based jobs dominated, while low and unskilled workers in the industrial heartland are being left behind.

In the Post-Industrial era, services and knowledge-based jobs dominated, while low and unskilled workers in the industrial heartland are being left behind.

In the new millennium, futurists and tech leaders now foresee the end of work itself for much of the population. In their vision, technology and artificial intelligence will fill in for much of what workers do now. The gainfully employed will be those largely running the new technology economy, with goods increasingly flowing from the countries.

## TECHNOLOGY IS CHANGING THE NATURE OF WORK

Many jobs and occupations have already been reduced and more frequently changed by the rise of new technologies, and this trend is expected to accelerate as artificial intelligence finds commercial applications. Estimates of how many jobs will change and how many on net will be lost vary widely, ranging from up to 47 percent of U.S. jobs within twenty years[77] to almost "all of the above" hyped in more than one start-up venture funding pitch.

Other analysts are more optimistic. In a series of detailed studies by occupation and by country, McKinsey Global Institute[78] concludes that some jobs will in fact become redundant as has been the case with every other economic transformation in the past, but at far lower rates than the doomsday projections. Their studies estimate that 5 percent of current occupations in the U.S. can be fully automated, and that another 60 percent could see at least 30 percent of their activities automated using currently demonstrated technology. While these shifts will produce changes in how work is organized along with the overall mix of jobs available, more jobs will likely be created than lost for the very same reasons that the job universe has expanded in every other economic transformation the U.S. has gone through.

Doomsday projections over the threat of technology are not new. As one of his examples of how capitalism inevitably destroys the livelihood of workers, Marx[79] predicted that the power loom would replace all weavers. They're still with us, producing far more per worker using machines at far lower prices that enable workers all over the world to clothe their families.

## ARE WAGES TRULY STAGNATING?

Prior to the coronavirus, the U.S. economic expansion of the 2010s was distinguished for concentrating job growth at the higher and lower ends of the wage scale. There hasn't been the robust growth in middle class wage jobs that we have seen from prior recoveries. This has strong implications for opportunities for upward mobility when the bridge out of poverty and low incomes has been shrinking.

Wage stagnation is the reason the left argues for greater government control of the economy, wages, working conditions, and benefits. The trend in real hourly wages is one of the main data points used to justify the wage stagnation claim. Using this metric from the U.S. Bureau of Labor Statistics data, the real average hourly wage for production and nonsupervisory employees peaked in February 1973 and did not exceed this level again until January 2019.[80]

There are several problems with this conclusion. First, the "real wage" used in the stagnation analyses is calculated using the Consumer Price Index (CPI). The CPI measures how prices for a particular basket of goods and services have changed over time. For instance, the CPI is a good measure when considering how the price of a TV has changed. But a measure that is better at capturing the substitution effect is the Personal Consumption Expenditures Index (PCE)

> In a series of detailed studies by occupation and by country, McKinsey Global Institute, concludes that some jobs will in fact become redundant as has been the case with every other economic transformation in the past, but at far lower rates than the doomsday projections.

now used by the Federal Reserve as their preferred measure of inflation. Under this index, real hourly wages passed the 1973 level in late 1998,[81] and outside of the recessionary periods have grown more or less consistently since.

The results from the two measures are shown in Figure 15. Measured by CPI, average hourly wages can be said to have stagnated. Using the more realistic PCE, real wages instead have grown 22 percent since 1998.

**FIGURE 15. REAL (2018) HOURLY WAGE OF PRIVATE PRODUCTION AND NONSUPERVISORY EMPLOYEES, FEB 1973=100**

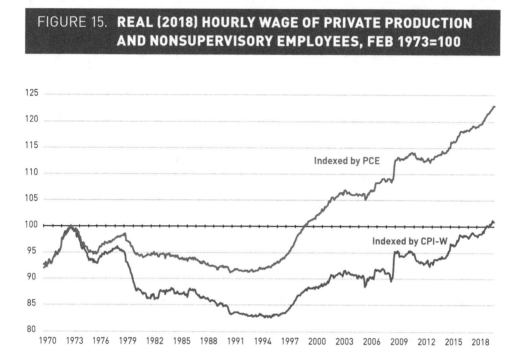

*Source: U.S. Bureau of Labor Statistics, U.S. Bureau of Economic Analysis, all data seasonally adjusted*

Second, using an average is not always a good measure. People constantly are moving in and out of the workforce. The average is affected by overall pay level, but also to a high degree by how many are coming in at starting positions and wage levels, and how many are leaving at the top of their scale. Donald Boudreaux[82] offers a good analogy. If you have three kids, the average height will generally increase over time. But if you suddenly bring a baby into the mix, the average goes down even though each kid likely is continuing to grow each year. They haven't become shorter. Your brood is just a different mix.

Labor force participation rates overall have dropped, going from a high of 67.1 percent in 1997 – 2000 to 62.9 percent in 2018, as youth rates plummeted, young adult and ages 55 and older softened, and ages 65 and older increased but not always at the same pay levels as their career jobs. The current aging of the Baby Boomer generation, leaving at the peak of their earning level, in particular is producing a major demographic shift in labor force composition. As these higher earners continue to leave and are replaced with new entrants, the dampening effect on wage statistics will continue for several years whether measured by averages or medians. Compounding this statistical effect is the continuing draw of workers back into the labor force by the economy's long-term growth prior to the coronavirus, including part time going to full time closer to the average or median wage but also those previously out of or marginally attached to the labor force coming back in at lower rates.[83]

## WHERE ARE TODAY'S JOBS?

More critical to wage and income issues is the distribution of jobs.

In the economic recovery of the 2010s, net job growth has been far more concentrated than in past recoveries, with the top four job categories accounting for nearly three-quarters of the total. This mix has a profound influence on the wage opportunities in our current economy. The top four cover mixed wage Health Care and higher wage Professional & Technical Services jobs, but with just under a third of net jobs coming from lower wage Food Services and Social Assistance jobs (largely driven by publicly-funded and minimum wage In-Home Supportive Service workers in California and five other large states).

The current aging
of the Baby Boomer
generation, leaving
at the peak of the
earning levels,
in particular is
producing a major
demographic shift
in labor force
composition.

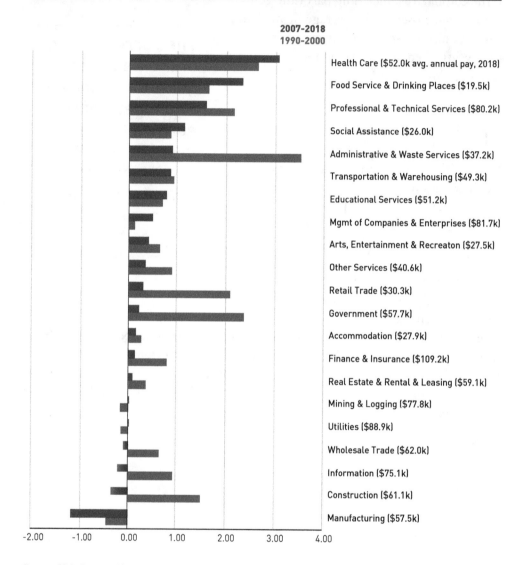

## FIGURE 16. STRUCTURAL CHANGE: 1990-2000 VS. 2007-2018 RECOVERIES BY NET JOBS

**2007-2018**
**1990-2000**

Health Care ($52.0k avg. annual pay, 2018)

Food Service & Drinking Places ($19.5k)

Professional & Technical Services ($80.2k)

Social Assistance ($26.0k)

Administrative & Waste Services ($37.2k)

Transportation & Warehousing ($49.3k)

Educational Services ($51.2k)

Mgmt of Companies & Enterprises ($81.7k)

Arts, Entertainment & Recreaton ($27.5k)

Other Services ($40.6k)

Retail Trade ($30.3k)

Government ($57.7k)

Accommodation ($27.9k)

Finance & Insurance ($109.2k)

Real Estate & Rental & Leasing ($59.1k)

Mining & Logging ($77.8k)

Utilities ($88.9k)

Wholesale Trade ($62.0k)

Information ($75.1k)

Construction ($61.1k)

Manufacturing ($57.5k)

-2.00    -1.00    0.00    1.00    2.00    3.00    4.00

*Source: U.S. Bureau of Labor Statistics; net change in nonfarm jobs (millions)*

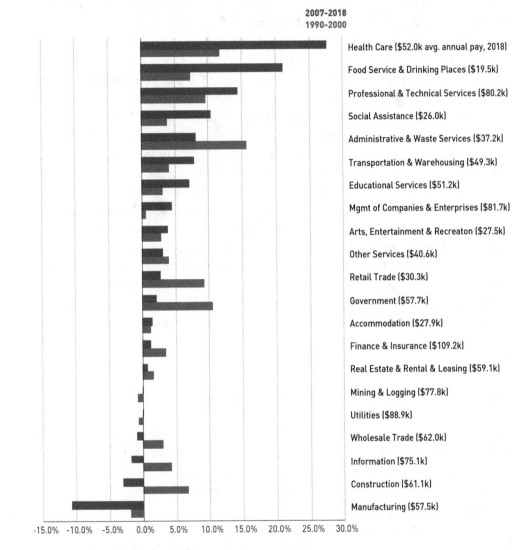

## FIGURE 17. STRUCTURAL CHANGE: 1990–2000 VS. 2007–2018 RECOVERIES, BY NET JOB SHARE

2007-2018
1990-2000

Health Care ($52.0k avg. annual pay, 2018)

Food Service & Drinking Places ($19.5k)

Professional & Technical Services ($80.2k)

Social Assistance ($26.0k)

Administrative & Waste Services ($37.2k)

Transportation & Warehousing ($49.3k)

Educational Services ($51.2k)

Mgmt of Companies & Enterprises ($81.7k)

Arts, Entertainment & Recreaton ($27.5k)

Other Services ($40.6k)

Retail Trade ($30.3k)

Government ($57.7k)

Accommodation ($27.9k)

Finance & Insurance ($109.2k)

Real Estate & Rental & Leasing ($59.1k)

Mining & Logging ($77.8k)

Utilities ($88.9k)

Wholesale Trade ($62.0k)

Information ($75.1k)

Construction ($61.1k)

Manufacturing ($57.5k)

-15.0%  -10.0%  -5.0%  0.0%  5.0%  10.0%  15.0%  20.0%  25.0%  30.0%

*Source: U.S. Bureau of Labor Statistics; net change in nonfarm jobs (percent of total)*

Considered by area, the stratification is even more pronounced. Using the annual jobs data, the top 25 (out of 389 total) metropolitan statistical areas (MSAs) account for 66 percent of the net job expansion in the economic expansion of the 2010s. In the 1990s, that same 66 percent of net jobs was instead shared by 122 MSAs. In all, only 59 MSAs by 2018 accounted for the same share of net job growth as all 389 MSAs (85 percent of the total) did in the 1990s.

Based on the national and MSA totals, micropolitan and rural areas gained 3.5 million jobs (15 percent of the total) in the 1990s. During the economic expansion of the 2010s, these areas as a group basically broke even on job creation, while 103 MSAs still showed job numbers below their pre-2008-09 recession levels (compared to only 7 MSAs in the 1990s) at the end of 2018. Job growth has not only been concentrated; many parts of the nation have been fully left behind.

In fact, wage levels are tied to the number and types of jobs we are creating. And the types of jobs being created are shaped by the competitive environment we face, often itself shaped by the public policies in effect.

The middle class saw an upsurge beginning in the 1950s because the U.S. was creating middle class wage jobs. The middle class grew throughout the country as these jobs dispersed, especially to previously poorer areas in the South and Intermountain West. But after many states and cities embraced service and subsequently high tech jobs, and began shaping their competitive environment accordingly through regulation and tax and education policies, the less educated and the less skilled have found their options more limited to jobs at the lower end of the wage scale.

## MINIMUM WAGE IS NOT THE PROBLEM, IT'S INCOME

The debate around wages also misses the point that it is household income that really matters. A $15 an hour minimum wage is far less effective if there are only part time jobs offering 20 hours a week at this level, compared to a $12 an hour, full time job. Instead, those on the political left seek to use the wage data in pushing for higher minimum wage.[84]

Minimum wage jobs historically have played an important economic role. Requiring lower skill sets or those that can easily be acquired through on-the-job training, these have been important gateway jobs for youth and immigrants, helping them to develop basic workplace skills that prepare them for better paying future jobs and thereby increasing their lifetime earnings.[85] They have also been a source of supplemental income for many households, whether part-time or summer gigs for students or part-time and seasonal work for seniors and for secondary household wage earners.

In fact, most minimum wage jobs are not held by the poor. A 2014 Congressional Budget Office analysis[86] of a then-proposed hike in the federal minimum wage from $7.25 to $10.10 concluded that only 19 percent of the resulting wage increases would benefit families below the poverty income, while 29 percent would go to families earning more than three times the poverty level. The more recent 2019 Congressional Budget Office review[87] of a proposed raise to $15 an hour indicates that about 40 percent of the potentially affected low wage earners are in families earning more than three times poverty income.

This wage agenda is fundamentally mired in the doomsday projections over the future of work, those who see an inevitable future chasm between the rich and the poor caused by automation and technology. The debate should not be over making minimum wage jobs comfortable for the workers they see as being left behind. The debate instead should be focused on a key question: are we creating enough jobs at the right wage levels to enable workers to move beyond minimum wage incomes? Are they being prepared with the skills needed to move up? Are we creating the conditions required to keep the U.S. competitive for the better paying jobs in the future? Are we keeping open paths for upward mobility or instead locking in policies that will create the class divides that hamper the economies and societies in much of the rest of the world?

> **The debate instead should be focused on a key question: are we creating enough jobs at the right wage levels to enable workers to move beyond minimum wage incomes?**

Using a general rule-of-thumb rule for middle class as median income plus and minus 50 percent and acknowledging that the data only covers money income, the most recent Census results can be apportioned through their income groupings as follows: (1) lower income at $0 to $24,999, (2) middle income at $25,000 to $99,999, and (3) higher income at $100,000 and above. The shifting mix between these income groups is shown in Figure 18. Again, the income definition in the data is money income, and does not incorporate the other income factors such as the effects of capital gains, non-cash government assistance, value of employee benefits and federal retiree benefits, and taxes. The data also uses real household income as determined by CPI-U-RS[88] rather than the PCE Index. These considerations aside, the results shown in Figure 18 suggest some general conclusions.

First, the middle class has shrunk, going from 62 percent of households in 1972 to just over 50 percent in 2018. Movement, however, was primarily out of the middle and into the higher income group, which doubled from 15 percent to 30 percent in this period. The lower income group on the other hand was less changed in this period, going from 23 percent to 19 percent, largely reflecting the failures of the existing programs begun under the War on Poverty. As reported by the Census Bureau based on the CPI-U-RS, real median household money income grew 21 percent in this period. Adjusting to the PCE Index, real median income expanded 36 percent.

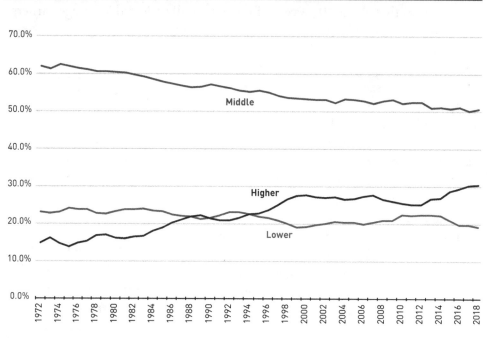

FIGURE 18. **DISTRIBUTION OF HOUSEHOLDS BY INCOME GROUP**

*Source: Census Bureau, Income and Poverty in the United States: 2018*

A key factor in this shift is the declining—in both absolute and relative terms—of historic middle-class wage jobs, in particular blue-collar jobs in industries such as manufacturing and resource extraction as discussed earlier.

There has been a tremendous change in labor force skills, as illustrated in Figure 19.[89] Our economy has gone from one where high school was the defining gateway to a good paying job to the standard today, a college degree. The share of adults with degrees has risen more than three-fold from 10.6 percent in 1990 to 35 percent in 2018.

FIGURE 19. **EDUCATIONAL ATTAINMENT DISTRIBUTION, AGE 25+**

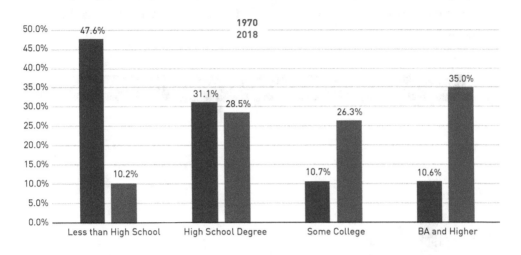

*Source: Census Bureau, 1970 Census, 2017 American Community Survey*

Figure 19 also shows that the proportion of the U.S. population with a high school diploma has not changed, and some 10 percent still don't have that level of education. Progress in the fight against poverty or even policies to improve household incomes other than through outright cash transfers are simply unattainable unless skills improvement within these portions of the labor force are addressed.

The economy has good paying jobs available at this level—if workers have the proper training. Rather than a college degree, vocational training, certification, and licensing as a route to skills development still gets plumbers to average annual wages of $58,150, radiation therapists to $86,730, and even the Homer Simpsons of the world (nuclear power operators) to $95,310.[90]

Higher pay opportunities remain within many industries. Figure 20 shows the average annual wage for these educational levels in the traditional blue-collar industries—ranging from $52,000 in Transportation & Warehousing to $95,400 in Utilities for high school diploma holders and $46,500 to $88,000 in the same industries for those who did not finish. But as blue-collar industries shrink in relative size, the fastest growing replacement jobs are paying on average from $24,100 in Food Service & Drinking Places to $45,500 in Health Care for high school graduates and from $22,500 to $41,600 to high school dropouts. Figure 20 also shows the share of employment in each industry by educational level to indicate the extent to which the blue-collar part of the economy has been a source of jobs for these workers.

Higher paying jobs are also provided at this educational level in Professional, Scientific & Technical Services if workers are armed with the necessary skills, but the three industries constituting the primary job replacement opportunities shown in Figure 20 provide nearly five times as many jobs at this level and growing.

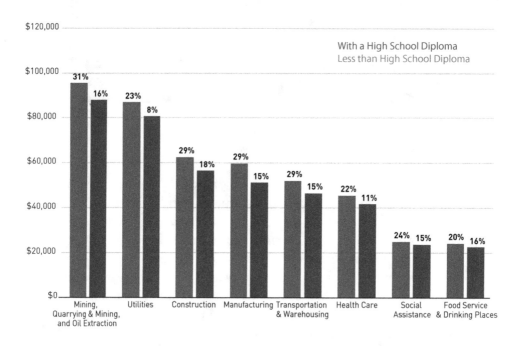

FIGURE 20. **AVERAGE WAGE & SHARE OF INDUSTRY EMPLOYMENT**

With a High School Diploma
Less than High School Diploma

*Source: U.S. Census Bureau, Quarterly Workforce Indicators, 2018 (from state data)*

For workers overall, however, skills training equals pay and pay equals the ability to acquire assets and move towards income stability. As seen in Figure 21, the jump in pay associated with educational attainment is not so much a dividing line as it is across a fairly substantial income chasm. The difference in average salary between workers with a Bachelor's degree and those with an AA is close to the median annual costs of owning a home (including mortgage, taxes, insurance, and utilities).[91] The difference between having a Bachelor's degree and only a high school diploma is about a third more.

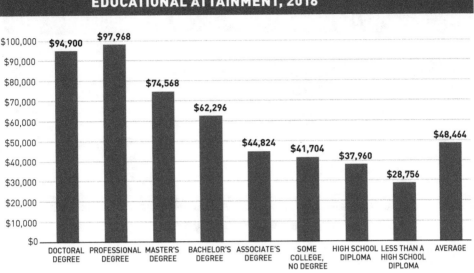

**FIGURE 21. AVERAGE ANNUAL EARNINGS BY EDUCATIONAL ATTAINMENT, 2018**

*Source: U.S. Bureau of Labor Statistics*

Within traditional blue-collar jobs, however, conditions are changing. As manufacturing becomes more automated, workers will require a higher level of technical skills to remain competitive. If products move from traditional technology to those envisioned under the "Green New Deal," actual reductions in jobs are likely. For instance, the labor hours required to produce a higher-priced electric vehicle (EV) are estimated to be 30 percent less than the often-unionized hours required to produce a traditional internal combustion engine-powered vehicle.[92] And many of the critical components to build them, including the battery pack that typically makes up 40-50 percent of an EV's cost, are not made by U.S. workers but come from highly concentrated producers in East Asia and even more concentrated raw material sources in Africa, China, and South America.

Both mining and utilities are under regulatory siege in some states and cities, as activists seek to reduce if not all out eliminate oil and gas. As traditional power plants are replaced by fewer and lower paid jobs at wind and solar farms—someone hired to wash down solar panels simply isn't paid at the same scale as a worker, often unionized, who maintains high pressure piping. Even in construction, a full time as well as fallback job for many households in these groupings, increasing the use of project labor agreements and expanding prevailing wage requirements in some areas serve as guild protections limiting access for many workers.

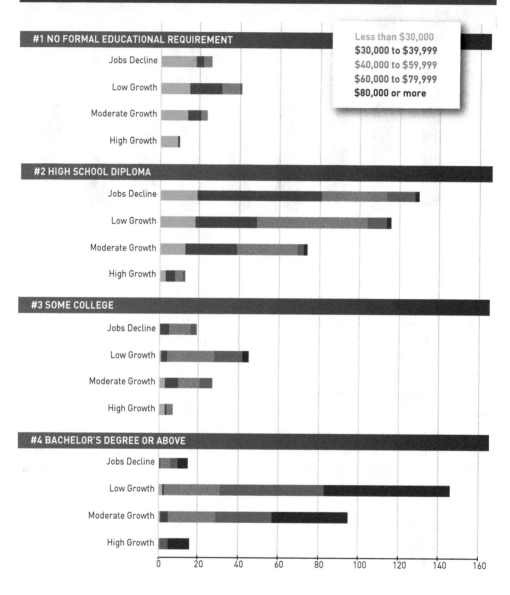

FIGURE 22. **PROJECTED NUMBER OF OCCUPATIONS BY TYPICAL ENTRY-LEVEL EDUCATION REQUIREMENT, PROJECTED JOBS GROWTH 2018-28 & MEDIAN PAY 2018**

Less than $30,000
**$30,000 to $39,999**
$40,000 to $59,999
**$60,000 to $79,999**
**$80,000 or more**

**#1 NO FORMAL EDUCATIONAL REQUIREMENT**
Jobs Decline
Low Growth
Moderate Growth
High Growth

**#2 HIGH SCHOOL DIPLOMA**
Jobs Decline
Low Growth
Moderate Growth
High Growth

**#3 SOME COLLEGE**
Jobs Decline
Low Growth
Moderate Growth
High Growth

**#4 BACHELOR'S DEGREE OR ABOVE**
Jobs Decline
Low Growth
Moderate Growth
High Growth

0    20    40    60    80    100    120    140    160

*Source: U.S. Bureau of Labor Statistics*

Combining regulatory and other competitive pressures on the traditionally higher paid jobs along with higher skill demands in many occupations, the demand outlook for these educational levels is mixed but show a more pronounced downward trend for the lowest-skilled. The most recent occupational projections (conducted before the coronavirus pandemic affected the U.S. economy) through 2028 by the U.S. Bureau of Labor Statistics (Figure 22) show the typical education level expected by employers for entry-level hires. The primary moderate growth (5,000 to 49,999 jobs over the period) and low growth (0 to 4,999 jobs) occupations for workers without a high school diploma fall into the less than $30,000 to $39,999 median annual pay (2018 level) range. High school graduates face a wider range of occupational choices with mixed wage opportunities, but far fewer options in the high growth (more than 50,000 jobs) category than projected for those with a college degree. High school graduates also show by far the greatest number of occupations with projected declines, including a substantial number of higher pay jobs.

Based on these projections, jobs will still be there for those with a high school degree or less, and there will still be higher pay opportunities if they acquire the necessary skills. There will, however, be substantial shrinkage of higher pay occupations as well, and the available replacements are just as likely to be lower paid as not if their skills are not adequate.

## GIG JOBS

Most concerns over the future of work center around the extent to which the basic employment model itself is changing.

As U.S. businesses have sought to remain competitive within a globalizing economy and remain in play with competition from China, Mexico, and other lower cost producers, they have turned to revamping their cost structures including through greater use of contract labor and services and temporary workers. In doing so, businesses have gained greater control of costs throughout their market cycles, while often obtaining higher quality results through cost and knowledge efficiencies offered by contracting out. This particularly benefits small businesses who simply cannot afford to maintain the regulatory compliance, legal, human resources, and other administrative structures now required to operate in this country.

Most notably, as high tech has taken on new industries for disruption, their models have relied on gaining significant cost advantages by foregoing traditional wage and salary workforces and instead competing through the use of gig workers paid by the task. In essence, this is the return of piece workers associated more with the beginning stages of economic development rather than developed economies where they are now becoming more known.

The actual number of gig workers as that term is actually much lower than you might imagine. In a series of questions first included in the 2017 survey, Bureau of Labor Statistics estimated[93] there were 1.6 million electronically mediated workers accounting for only 1.0 percent of total employment. Of this 1.6 million, 44 percent did their work entirely online, while 62 percent did this work in person, as is the case for ride-share drivers. Note there is an overlap in these amounts which accounts for persons who worked in both situations.

Distributed by educational attainment (Figure 23), those with a high school diploma or less were more likely to do this work in person, while nearly two-thirds of the online work was done by those with a college degree. In person jobs were a much greater source of work for African-Americans (23.0 percent of in person jobs compared to 12.1 percent of all jobs in the economy) and somewhat higher for Latinos (18.5 percent versus 16.6 percent), while whites held a higher relative share of online jobs (84.0 percent versus 78.7 percent) and Asians only somewhat higher (7.0 percent versus 5.9 percent).[94]

## FIGURE 23. DISTRIBUTION OF GIG WORKERS (%) BY WORK LOCATION, 2017

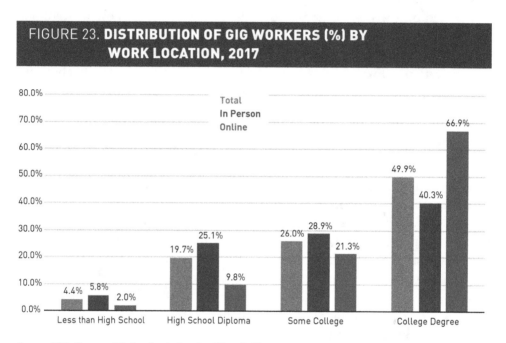

*Source: U.S. Bureau of Labor Statistics, Age 25 and older*

While the Bureau cautions about the use of the recoded data on this factor, about three-quarters of these workers did so as their main job. The remainder used this work as a second job or as a source of additional pay.

Moreover, the popular notion of gig jobs becoming a dominant source of somehow "inferior" jobs just does not show up in the overall employment numbers. As indicated in Figure 24 (which indexes both full-time and part-time employment to their January 2000 levels), part-time employment took a major jump as full-time jobs fell during the 2008-09 recession as workers sought any type of employment, including going out and working on their own. Before the coronavirus halted the continued expansion of the U.S. economy during the 2010s, full-time employment constituted more than all of the subsequent expansion when measured on a net basis. Between June 2009 and September 2019, U.S. Bureau of Labor data indicated full-time employment (seasonally adjusted; working 35 hours a week or more) grew by 18.3 million, while part-time (under 35 hours) shrank by 0.4 million.

With the latest data showing only 6 percent of part-time workers doing so because they could only find part-time work, gig jobs obviously have not yet risen beyond the point where they are an option rather than the only choice. Viewed from this perspective, the growth in part-time employment was an economic survival response during the 2008-09 recession (and will likely be so again due to the coronavirus-related recession). The numbers remain elevated primarily because of individual worker choice. Gig jobs from this perspective did not force a new working paradigm on the economy, but instead was one of the options that made these outcomes possible.

## FIGURE 24. **EMPLOYMENT BY HOURS WORKED, JAN 2000=100**

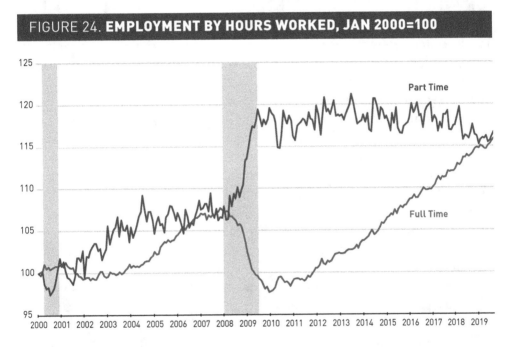

Source: *U.S. Bureau of Labor Statistics*

Regardless of their scale, gig jobs have gone from a work option with more earning potential to the symbol of all that is wrong with current work trends.

At the extreme, California recently became the first state to push back against the gig worker model, passing legislation[95] to reclassify many of these workers from contractors to employees. They even went further by going beyond gig workers alone and instead—except for the politically favored few able to secure individual exemptions in the legislation—enacted provisions affecting the status of many in the much larger universe of workers in contingent and alternative work situations. The bill, however, has yet to survive potential legal and initiative/referendum challenges. It remains to be seen whether this approach of legislating against innovation is just the last gasp of the previous century's job model, rather than a sign of things to come.

There is a decided difference in how these jobs should be viewed in context of household welfare, especially for lower income households. If choosing a gig job is a personal choice, then it will provide a high level of benefit whether it is a good way to become more employable in the future, allow flexibility in one's daily schedule, generate a supplemental but dependable source of income, or will simply let one become their own boss. The broader contingent/alternative data shows many of these workers are doing it from choice and would rather work this way than under other arrangements.

## FOR WHOM THE CHANGE TOLLS

For those prepared with the necessary skills, changes in the work environment provide flexible options in how and where work is conducted, with compensation models that better reflect individual and household needs whether at the beginning, middle, or slowing down phase of their working life. For others, the diminishing supply of long-term jobs with full benefits is occurring at the same time that this country continues to erect competitive barriers that limit creation of new jobs of comparable value to all but those with a higher education.

Getting a high school diploma used to be a celebration event, the acquisition of the basic pass to a middle-class life. For too many today, there's little difference between getting a diploma and dropping out. Unless they're one of the favored who have been prepared to go on to college, a high school diploma means far less in the current and evolving jobs market. Without other skills training, the graduate and the dropout are just as equally qualified for a minimum wage job.

Even if the concept of a life-long job with full benefits is now less evident than in the past, it has been an option since the 1950s for many if that was what they sought and if they acquired and maintained the skills necessary to secure it. This option still remains but is also under constant threat from the trends of globalization and disruption risks from a tech industry still looking for new ways to grow.

The middle class is shrinking, but it is because many households have moved up in educational attainment and the better incomes it provides. Those in the middle and lower incomes have not so much fallen behind as have been left behind by competitive conditions that favor better paying job creation for those with a degree rather than those with a diploma or less.

The jobs being created in the U.S. are also changing. Before the coronavirus impacted the U.S. economy, venture capital in China, India, and other rapid growth economies was focused on growing a middle class, creating the goods production and goods movement jobs that provide a decent wage to the broadest possible range of educational skills. Having created the consumer and educational base from those middle-class jobs, these venture capital sources now are turning to services and high tech. They are maintaining the pace of their other investments knowing full well that, while services and tech may be the jobs of the future, jobs for their full populations are needed now.

Venture capital in this country instead focuses unduly on two types of jobs – those requiring a Bachelor's degree or higher, or warehouse and delivery jobs to deliver the goods now produced overseas. In the process, public schools as they now operate are no longer the great tool of expanded opportunity they became under the High School Movement. Instead, they have become a winnowing process, sorting out those who can go on to college and succeed and those without employable skills left to struggle on their own or on government assistance.

## MORE GOVERNMENT CONTROL IS NOT THE ANSWER

The appeal of greater government control of the economy has always been at its strongest when its purveyors have been successful in convincing a population it is divided into haves and have-nots. The rhetoric coming from those in the 2020 campaign cycle who are now test-driving the label "social democrat" if not full on "socialist" seeks to deepen this divide.

The nation's transformations in the past always arose from a more inclusive spirit. The fundamental goals were more egalitarian in seeking to increase opportunity through education. Through a more educated workforce, we could create a greater income base that would make upward mobility possible for a greater share of the population. Some would always make more and some less, but the end result was the betterment of all communities because the drive came from the bottom up.

The current prescriptions coming from those who truly believe the Piketty analysis of our ills—regardless of whether it is right or not—would upend this historical path to progress. Rather than actions to prepare workers for the future, they would instead seek to hold it back through greater government control and dispensation of jobs, wages, and even worker incomes. Instead of seeking to make our economy more competitive and more capable of providing jobs to the full range of its workforce, these proposals and others like the Green New Deal would destroy far more middle class wage jobs than what has been achieved to date by globalization, or even what could be envisioned in the grandest disruption dreams of the tech industry.

# CHAPTER SEVEN
## Skills-Based Economics

My early life began on a platform shaped by the expectations laid out by the poverty programs. Our neighborhood in that small Texas town was poor. We were expected to remain poor and require help from the programs for the rest of our lives.

My mother raised the platform higher. As the first in her family to go to college, she expected that her children would go as well. That led to my college education where I attained skill sets to go out and start my own business and begin the process of building generational wealth. That has afforded me an opportunity to own my own home, pay for my own health care, send my daughter to a good school, pay for her college, and prepare for retirement with dignity. It also meant creating jobs for other people and having the resources and time to give back through public service, including helping other young people raise their expectations as well. Football opened doors for me, and there are not enough words to express the extent of my gratitude for that chance. But my focus was on being a good student because it was clear which skills were going to carry me for the longer term.

The platform has now been raised even higher for my daughters not only through expectations with a higher goal but also with a base of resources to help them succeed.

This was, and for most people still is, the American Dream. It's why so many came to this country and continue to do so. They didn't come here for a handout; they came here to work and build a better future for their families. For many, this meant building their own business and, by doing so, control their own destiny. It's what's kept many workers and many families going even as they fell behind in the Great Recession and continue to struggle in still too many areas of our country.

Public policy now serves to keep too many on that first platform through dependence on government assistance. Before the coronavirus, too many of the promises from the 2020 Democratic presidential candidates, including universal basic income, would condemn many more there as well.

We need to stop thinking about our economic future in doomsday terms. Those predictions have always been there. They have never come to pass. America must return to what has kept this country moving ahead and to an even better way of life, namely thinking in terms of the possible. The currents working against this vision must be viewed instead as challenges to be overcome in moving our economy ahead for all. What can we do to provide greater opportunities? What do we need to do to get there? And what do we need to do to position our greatest resource, our people, to raise up this platform for success?

## IT'S EDUCATION

One of the main reasons why we have such a large current wage gap is the performance of our schools. As pointed out by Alan Greenspan,[96] in the immediate decades following World War II, wage growth at all educational levels largely tracked along the same path due to various factors affecting labor supply at each level. As a result of the training they received, many veterans left the Armed Forces with marketable skills commanding relatively higher wages in what was then still largely an industrial economy. The rapid growth in workers with college degrees—first as a result of the GI Bill and subsequently through its effect on generational expectations—produced an upsurge in supply that moderated overall wage growth at this level even as demand for degreed workers rose.

This wage distribution remained stable in large part because schools continued to prepare workers as the economy needed them and at the level required. College preparation expanded for those choosing to continue along that path. For others, a high school diploma often meant valuable vocational skills. For all graduates, it was a certification of a core level of proficiency in language/communication and math skills essential as technology applications rose in many better paying occupations. The schools worked, and their students went on to expected wage levels because they were prepared.

The value of a high school diploma was such that there is even a period where it appears to have replaced college degrees as a ticket to better paying jobs. Using data developed by Claudia Goldin and Lawrence Katz,[97] college graduation rates peaked in the mid-1940s and declined over the next decade. High school graduation rates, on the other hand, saw one of their steepest rises in this period. While other factors are in play during this time, this situation suggests that ". . . the economic value of a high school diploma was such that graduates did not feel the need to pursue college."[98]

The wholesale elimination of vocational training combined with a dramatic drop in proficiency levels meant that a high school diploma was now more a winnowing process than its previous role as a ticket to success. The students who could succeed and reach higher wage levels would go on to secure the new base requirement of a college degree. Those who the schools have failed—an increasing share of the overall labor force—were now finding jobs that paid roughly the same level for those with a diploma as for those who dropped out.

> **One of the main reasons why we have such a large current wage gap is the performance of our schools.**

Debating the issues over wage growth are meaningless if schools are failing in their basic job of preparing students to operate successfully in the economy.

## THE FUNDAMENTALS

Key to eliminating the wage gap, lifting people out of poverty and expanding economic opportunity for all is a concept that I call skills-based economics.

Skills-based economics is centered on empowering the individual. Just as labor mobility has enabled the U.S. to adjust more rapidly to technology changes in the past, labor adaptability will be essential for workers to adjust to shifting occupational demands, changing job structures, new entrepreneurial opportunities now made possible under the current wave of technology innovation and the uncertainty presented by the gig economy.

Skills-based economics suggest every person can learn a skill producing a decent income through wages or starting off on their own, becoming an entrepreneur either in the big "E" sense of having the next billion-dollar IPO idea or in the little "e" sense of a family business with maybe a few workers to provide both income security and a sense of independence. The challenge to declining job security is to create the structures that enable workers to acquire the skills needed to adapt to changing occupational needs or to create their own job.

This is not a new concept. It's how our country—alone among nations—has repeatedly led in the past. The Common Schools Movement equipped the U.S. with the most broadly skilled and productive work force throughout most of the 19th century as we grew from an agrarian and resource base to an industrial economy. The High School Movement did the same in the first half of the 20th century as we led in industrial production and the economy broadened to trades and white-collar jobs. The GI Bill took a generation previously under threat of being made economically obsolete by the Great Depression and expanded the skills base, making possible a growing economy that turned more to science, engineering, and services. The upsurge in college enrollment beginning in the mid-1950s created the skills base that produced the information-based industries that lead our economy today.

Skills development has often been viewed as something coming after economic disruption or transformation. Jobs are created; workers have to be trained to fill them. Federal training programs run on the model of workers being retrained to fill whatever opportunities remain after their jobs are destroyed. Our economic history shows the opposite. Skills have been advanced and over a broader base in each iteration. Innovation came as creativity was released. Jobs and wages increased as the newly skilled formed their own businesses if not entirely new industries.

This is not a conclusion based on some socialist theory of labor value, but rather is a reflection of how our country has grown, prospered, and spread that prosperity over an ever-growing share of the population. That growth is now at risk by those who fundamentally believe that many simply are not capable of keeping up in an increasingly technological world.

A focus on skills as a driving force does not mean everybody needs to go to college. There are good paying jobs now that require less than a college degree. They will still be there in the future. But they will not necessarily be slots where the skills can be picked up on the job. They will require training of the type we once broadly had in our high schools and now has shifted to community colleges and trade schools. Often, these jobs will require a separate level of certification and licensing.

Skill demands will also change over time, and if the past few decades are any indication, will do so at an accelerating rate. Historically, colleges approached education from a dual purpose—instilling a level of expertise within a given discipline but also teaching students how to learn. They developed the capacity for life-long learning and individual adaptation. Skills training at levels other than college need to embrace this concept as well, going beyond the tendency of the public training programs to operate simply as certificating mills, churning out whatever training is needed for the occupations in demand at the time.

We do not need to warehouse a large part of our workforce as would happen under UBI. We need to prepare them, engage them, and empower them to succeed. And by constantly improving the skills base, we can maintain the competitive conditions that in the past have spawned new technologies, new industries, and new job opportunities in a constantly changing world.

# A NEW SCHOOLS MOVEMENT: FROM K-12 TO K-14

The increasing skills that will be required for the jobs of the future cannot be achieved with the current state of our public schools. Just as the Common Schools Movement prepared the U.S. workforce for the 19th century economy, the High School Movement for industrialization, and expansion of college for the later 20th century, the workforce required for the evolving technology economy will require a higher level of skills that could be made possible through K-14.

K-14 does not mean simply adding two more years. It is a restructuring of public education so that students leave school either bound for college or holding a certificate of license for a trade or occupation.

In the current work environment, there is little difference in the prospects between those with only a high school diploma or graduate equivalent development (GED) credentials and those who drop out. Both are equally qualified for the same minimum wage jobs. A 2002 *City Journal* article noted that, "Nobel Prize-winning economist James Heckman and colleague Stephen Cameron have found GED holders to be 'statistically indistinguishable' from high school dropouts: they're not significantly more likely to land a job or to have higher hourly wages."[99]

Instead of being handed just a diploma, everyone instead should leave their education with a certificate, license for a trade or skill, or have an Associate's degree to guarantee transfer to a 4-year school. Those completing the 12th grade requirements should still have the option of going directly to a 4-year school, but even in today's everybody-gets-a-trophy world, the schools should be issuing diplomas that have meaning in the jobs market, which they currently do not.

K-14 should not just mean more years and more classrooms. It needs to be a restructuring of public education around the requirements set by the end goals of an AA certificate/license, AA for transfer, or 4-year enrollment for all students. A significant apprenticeship component should be included as well. In my run for mayor of Long Beach, this concept resonated deeply and personally with low income parents desperate for ways to keep their children in school, off the streets, and away from gangs. Our current system of apprenticeships is far too limited. In many states, apprenticeships are available through the unions. There are successes such as the programs run by the building trades unions, but there are also many more areas which could be expanded through other models. Even technical areas such as computer coding become an art once the basics are learned and can be taught as well or better through experience. Upper income families use their contacts to arrange internships that allow their children to be exposed to the vast array of careers. Apprenticeships expand this opportunity to families at all incomes.

The K-14 structure should also form the foundation for adult education. All current federal training dollars could be consolidated into a single state block grant for this purpose. Instead of the perennial efforts to better coordinate the many and forever-expanding federal programs, the funds should be consolidated and left to the states on how best to manage them.

## FREE COLLEGE IS NOT THE ANSWER

One policy option gaining in popularity is the notion of free college. This world-view holds that only the college educated gain substantially higher incomes and lower unemployment. With free college for all, the thinking goes, we can prepare more to find meaningful work without imposing crushing debt.

But this approach offers yet another cruel bait-and-switch promising economic advancement. Not every good paying job requires a college degree. Free college does nothing for those job seekers. Even if everybody in the labor force had a degree, it would mean little if the jobs are not there. Meanwhile, "progressive" policies that typically accompany the push for free college—higher taxes, more regulations and restrictions, and expanded government takeovers of private sector activity—mean those jobs will not necessarily be there even with free college.

Most important, free college means nothing if students are not prepared for it.[100] Instead of preparing students for the future, K-12 schools are now run largely as a winnowing process, concentrating on those students who will go on to college and succeed and, except for those states who have upped their investments in vocational training reforms, leaving the remainder to fend for themselves.

This mismatch is best illustrated by California's Utopian progressive vision. Once committed to free or nearly free higher education in the 1960s, California at that time also had public K-12 schools that by and large worked. That system helped lead to the burst of creativity resulting in the expansion and creation of jobs in endeavors as diverse as agriculture, transportation, electronics, aerospace, and even today's technology sector.

California has also embraced the current free college policy trend and has made some moves back towards more free tuition. Starting in 2017 and expanding in 2019, the state now provides up to two years of free tuition in the community colleges.[101] Tuition will be free, but the state has done nothing to control the high living costs that deter many from using it and attending college full time.[102] More critically, nothing has been done to prepare more students so that they can succeed in college.

Figure 25 illustrates the current state of college preparation within California's K-12 schools. Despite massive increases in K-12 funding which has grown 61 percent since 2011-12 and 45 percent compared to the pre-2008-09 recession high in 2007-08,[103] only 42.7 percent of the most recent cohort graduated high school after successfully completing the coursework required for acceptance in the state's lower-cost public universities (University of California (UC) and California State University (CSU)). Another 15.5 percent failed to graduate at all, although some of these students are likely to go on to earn a GED.

It also indicates that these numbers vary dramatically according to economic status. Just over two-thirds of all students within the public K-12 system (which includes charter schools) are classified as socioeconomically disadvantaged (SED). This is not strictly an income designation and covers students whose family income qualifies them for free or reduced cost school lunch, where neither parent has a high school diploma, or migrant, homeless, or foster youth. SED students, however, show a college preparation rate at roughly half that for the non-SED students. SED students comprise the overwhelming bulk of the student body and presumably the bulk of the schools' focus. These numbers, however, suggest otherwise.

The numbers become even more stark when broken down by gender and selected race/ethnicity. Young men in particular show far lower preparation rates in all categories but approach criminally negligent levels in several of the SED groups. Some are still likely to pursue college at a community college, a course that on average takes about seven years to gain a bachelor's degree[104], and for the unprepared, generally more. Two free years with no other reforms will at best remedy the education they should have received in K-12, and at worst is just as likely to be the opening bid in a lifetime of student debt.

### FIGURE 25. CALIFORNIA 4-YEAR COHORT GRADUATION RATES, 2018-19

|  | Graduation Rate | UC/CSU Eligible Graduation Rate |
|---|---|---|
| Non-SED (31% of students) | 92.0% | 60.6% |
| Male | 90.8% | 55.2% |
| Female | 93.3% | 66.3% |
| SED (69% of students) | 81.1% | 34.6% |
| Male | 77.3% | 27.9% |
| Female | 85.0% | 41.6% |
| SED - Asian | 91.8% | 62.0% |
| Male | 90.1% | 55.9% |
| Female | 93.7% | 68.5% |
| SED - Latino | 81.0% | 33.5% |
| Male | 77.0% | 26.4% |
| Female | 85.1% | 40.8% |
| SED - White | 80.2% | 29.8% |
| Male | 76.7% | 24.0% |
| Female | 84.1% | 36.1% |
| SED - African-American | 74.5% | 26.7% |
| Male | 69.8% | 19.8% |
| Female | 79.2% | 33.7% |

*Source: California Department of Education*

The developments under the High School Movement led to an expansion of publicly funded skills training in comprehensive high schools composed of classical education for those going on to college and vocational training for those going on to work. In part, this dual track arose from the demand for these skills in a changing economy, but also as the result of reformers pushing the schools to teaching "life skills" especially as enrollment grew during the Great Depression due to new restrictions on youth employment. Reform in this period stemmed from impulses to make schools more of a democratizing instrument in reaction against the more "elitist" aspects of traditional academic courses, but also came as a push for a "*differential treatment of students, depending on perceived aptitudes and intelligence.*"[105]

The undemocratic underpinnings of these reforms led to the later rejection of the dual college-vocational track system, only to lead to college expectations for all and elimination of vocational options for those who needed them, just as our economy came under greater competition from other nations. The numbers in Figure 25 suggest that intentional tracking has been replaced by a de facto system produced from the failures of our K-12 schools, but without the compensating skills development that once prepared students for higher wage jobs.

The public schools have even failed to some degree for those certified as eligible to apply to the 4-year systems. Many instead have had to take remedial courses that do not count towards their degree, but still cost tuition and extend the number of years they have to pay.[106] Facing this rising problem in the California State University (CSU) system—only 19 percent graduate after four years and 57 percent after six years—the decision was made recently to do away with the remedial classes altogether.[107] While these students may get their degrees a year or two sooner, the question remains: Will they have the actual skills to compete for better paying jobs in the future?

The other aspect is that fewer students are choosing to go to college. As shown in Figure 26, total enrollment of students from the U.S. declined 8 percent since 2010. Incorporating the partially compensating rise in foreign students eases the loss to 6 percent.

## FIGURE 26. **HIGHER EDUCATION ENROLLMENT**

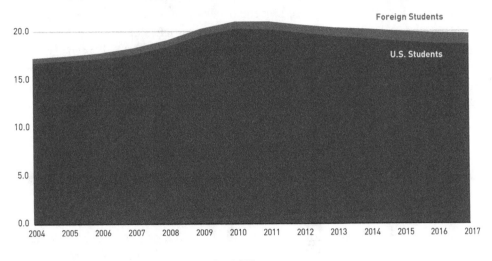

Foreign Students

U.S. Students

20.0

15.0

10.0

5.0

0.0

2004  2005  2006  2007  2008  2009  2010  2011  2012  2013  2014  2015  2016  2017

*Source: National Center for Education Statistics; Millions*

Free college alone does nothing to improve skills in these situations. It makes for a good soundbite, but it remains out of reach for the low income and many middle-income students the public schools have failed. It continues the progressive response of ignoring the source of the problems for fear of losing other members of their coalition, while offering some payment—in this case a totally inadequate payment—to those who have suffered the harm.

Skills training alone will not succeed in raising wages and incomes. Its prior success in this country came in tandem with a system of free enterprise that rewards innovation and individual initiative and provides the incentives to create jobs off an ever-improving skills base.

A counter example from socialist economies demonstrates this connection. Both the Soviet Union and currently Cuba set a priority on the training of a large cadre of medical professionals. Quality aside, they developed skills but only for service to the state. Even when these skills were turned into a service export, wages largely went to the state, not the skills-holder. Advances in medical knowledge and the quality of care consequently lagged in both countries, especially when compared to the West. The Soviets and Cuba developed the skills but eliminated opportunity and the chances for growth.

Just as incentivizing investment does not matter if there are no skilled entrepreneurs and workers to invest in, investing in skills does little to produce better incomes and overall growth if those personal incentives do not exist or are stopped in their tracks by a web of rules and taxes.

Free college and similar proposals are often promoted as progressive or populist. They are not. True populism means promoting policies that will benefit the individual and the people as a whole. Welfare, whether in its traditional form or under the guise of UBI, free college, or other "free" services from the government, does not. All it does is pay a part of the population to keep off the streets and ignore the harm caused by the other policies these advocates want to push. Jobs and self-reliance are replaced with government dependence. Standards of living fall as good jobs are replaced with aid and continue to fall as the government checks fail to keep up with costs. A future of opportunity is replaced with a future of rules. Such payments may smooth things over for a short period, but they do nothing to address wages and incomes in the long run or the generational effects.

## THE BUILDING BLOCKS OF SKILLS BASED ECONOMICS

My mom was sixteen years old when she gave birth to me. My dad died in a car accident three years later. Mom understood the value of parental involvement. She did not want the education system to merely pass me on but hold me accountable. She passed out cards with her name and phone number to the teachers, school janitors, cafeteria staff, and office administrators and told them to call her if they saw me misbehaving. She did not just hold out the promise of college. She made sure those years of schooling prepared me sufficiently to succeed.

In contrast, my uncles did not have that same daily encouragement and expectation to go to college. Predictably, they did not go. The schools where they grew up did not have enough resources to help remediate students like my uncles who struggled with academics. They got off track early and that undermined their education. We lived in a three-bedroom trailer without a quiet place to study. My grandparents lacked the education to help them with their homework. Inevitably they ended up with minimum wage jobs with no path to economic empowerment. Three of my uncles spent time in prison; two are unemployed and doing random work where they can find it.

The education system failed them by passing them on, grade after grade, until they got a diploma. The system did not give them a marketable skill set or even a realistic path that would take them beyond a minimum wage job and upward mobility.

My uncles' experience continues for too many today. The current K-12 system is incapable of producing the workforce required for the emerging economy. Rather than preparing all students, it now separates those who can acquire the needed skills from those the current progressive mindset would condemn to a life under universal basic income. Rather than a means for upward mobility, the K-12 schools have become in many places a process that cements the current income inequalities for generations. It is a system designed to feed a two-class society—those on universal basic income and those with high-value skills.

The current education policy proposals do little to change this situation. Advocates for universal preschool gloss over the fact that while there may be an initial benefit, the effects quickly dissipate once lower income students reach later grades.[108] Universal preschool would be largely a waste of funds unless preceded by reforms in K-12. The call for free college does not improve skills if students are unprepared. Free college simply sets up too many for frustration and failure unless K-12 prepares them for college.

# CHAPTER EIGHT
## Policy Reforms to Pave the Way for Economic Opportunity for All

One of the proudest moments of my life was creating a family trust. This is not meant to be elitist crowing, but it represents how far my family has been able to move beyond that trailer in rural Texas as the result of an education. It does not just represent my striving and my drive to get ahead but reflects that the struggle was as much to build a platform to raise the prospects for my children and their children and for every other generation to come. This is the inheritance that can be left to my children. The poverty of our past will be a source of humility and appreciation for my family from this point on rather than a cross for them to bear.

The path to generational wealth for every family begins with many of the elements laid out in this book.

Education is the essential. Breaking free of program dependence starts with changing expectations from a life of dependence to the opportunities made possible with a greater set of skills. As with my experience, once those expectations are raised, they will be passed on to every other generation to come.

The concept of portable benefits goes beyond just adjusting to a new world of work. It also means moving towards a system where workers own and control their own benefits. You don't own anything in Social Security. Regardless of how much you've paid into the system, you will get only so much each year and there is nothing to leave your family other than defined survivor options whether you draw monthly checks for thirty years or for only a few. You won't own any account under a UBI. You will get so much a year, and your children will likely be getting into line for the same amount as well. You don't own anything under a group benefit; the group does and if that group is government, it will determine what you get and when you get it. There is nothing to leave the next generation to help them improve their opportunities and escape the cycle of dependence.

Replacing the current poverty programs also means getting rid of their barriers to saving and accepting the responsibility of preparing for the future. Most programs have asset limits. Showing that you are "worthy" for government assistance means proving you are not saving for unforeseen emergencies, for school, for a home, and for your own retirement. The ultimate indignity awaits those families who have to strip their elderly loved ones of their remaining few assets in order to qualify for nursing homes under Medicaid. This situation is in the nature of welfare, that it should only go to those who truly need it. But for families caught in the generational cycle of dependence, it also means another set of rules that will keep them trapped forever.

Reform of occupational licensing and making regulations more responsive to competitive factors broaden opportunities to start a business. The adage that "you don't get rich working for someone else" does not automatically mean you will be working for yourself, but the independence and the chances to have a business to pass on is enough of a prospect that a great many people still want to try.

## TRANSFERABLE BENEFITS

The current system of employer-provided benefits now faces two challenges. As the value of those benefits has grown as a share of total compensation, there is a dampening effect on upward wage mobility particularly at the lower wage levels. When lower income California workers were asked to choose between a job with higher pay or a job with benefits, 59 percent preferred the benefits. The traditional process of wage growth through changing jobs is hindered as companies shift in the mix of benefits they pay. The other challenge comes from the changing nature of jobs. Workers today have a greater range of options in how and when they work. Many industries are moving to the independent contracting model, and few provide the same range of benefits found in traditional employment. Faced with the rising cost of competitive benefits, small businesses struggle to provide them for their employees, and this cost factor represents an additional hurdle to workers who want to start their own business.

Portable benefits offer a viable option in our changing workforce. Their benefits—whether they are health care, pensions, education, and childcare—follow the worker as they change jobs, gigs, or contracts throughout their working life. Contributions can come from both the employer and worker.

The basic structure for much of this system already exists, for example 401(k)s and other types of retirement accounts, health savings accounts, and flexible spending accounts, but most require modification to move from group benefits to the individual. Some progress in this regard has already been made, such as the Health Reimbursement Arrangements (HRA) created through regulation in 2019.[109] The recently-signed SECURE Act[110] opens greater flexibility for pension plans including annuities more akin to defined benefit models and greater use of Multiple Employer Plans (MEPs), although other provisions adopted with little debate strictly for offsetting revenue purposes severely reduce the operation of existing retirement options to serve also as a means of generational wealth creation.

> **A key principle in developing portable benefits first should be tax equity.**

The other challenge is funding. Most current proposals for portable benefits are based on the hiring firm or in the case of gig work the intermediary firm paying a set rate per gig into a central benefits account or similar arrangement. The issue of who pays, however, is in broad terms largely irrelevant. The worker one way or another ends up paying. Just as with the current employer-provided benefits, workers receive compensation in the form of wages/gig rate/contract rate and benefits. If benefits rise, less is available to increase wages. Similarly, if wages rise, less is available for benefits compensation, but workers now have higher incomes to acquire benefits on their own. For gig workers and independent contractors, the pay rates they are able to secure will consequently depend on the size of any such benefits rate. The key factor, though, is the extent to which centralized funds can provide benefits at a lower cost through bulk buying and risk diversification than what individuals can do on their own. The paths to getting there, moreover, rely in many cases on relaxing long-standing anti-monopoly restrictions on cooperation between employers.

A key principle in developing portable benefits first should be tax equity. If benefits now have a tax preference whether they come from an employer or are available to the self-employed, they should have the same tax treatment as if individuals acquire them on their own. Health insurance is not taxed if it comes from an employer plan, welfare, bought by someone running their own business, or for many taxpayers from Medicare. Someone buying insurance on their own should be treated the same way. Government should not be concerned with how the benefits flow. If it gives preferred tax treatment to one component or one form of employment, that should be available to all. There will always be issues of budget affordability. If offsetting savings are needed, there are more than enough programs to find them. The primary driver should instead be enabling opportunity and work that produces the general revenues to begin with.

A second principle is that there should be some level of transferability between accounts. Needs change as the stage of life changes. Cost projections don't always work out to the last decimal. Existing tools such as flexible spending accounts are severely limited both by cumbersome and costly administrative procedures and the absence of rollover provisions.

The final principle is to recognize that these are new work models. Some people do and will prefer them. They want the flexibility and sense of independence that self-employment provides, and many have already made substantial investments in order to compete and make this the source of their life's income. Others will continue to prefer the traditional models.

Rather than develop the benefit structures that enable these options, much of the legislation proposed and even passed to date seeks to shut them down. California's recent action[111] in this regard essentially prohibits—except for the politically favored few able to secure a carve-out in the bill—work models that state's economy pioneered. Others such as efforts in Seattle[112] and other cities seek to simply mandate benefit requirements without fully addressing the questions of financing or costs. Legislation in the state of Washington[113], and laws already enacted in California, Connecticut, Illinois, Maryland, and Oregon,[114] instead turn to public models and mandate employers to participate in publicly-created pension funds, with little regard to the historical performance of the public funds and their consequent financial model that depends on diverting tax revenues away from public services to mounting pension debts.

## REGULATION FOR THE 21ST CENTURY

Regulatory structures built for an industrial economy cannot provide the clarity, coordination, and timeliness of decisions in an economy of goods whose product life-cycles are measured in months and services that change each time operating systems update and make far more possible. Instead, they need to be more adaptive and responsive if jobs are to be available for newly skilled workers. Creativity and entrepreneurship by these workers need to be encouraged and rewarded, not stopped in their steps by a blanket of ever-expanding fees, taxes, and rules.

Current efforts provide a much-needed period of relief from the results of the previous decades. The most recent Federal Register in total for 2019 contains the smallest number of rules since records started being kept in the mid-1970s, following the second lowest in 2017 and third lowest in 2018.[115] These numbers are even more notable when considering that many of the rules issued in this period were modernizing of outdated provisions or repeals of those that no longer apply to today's conditions.

More, however, still needs to be done but should start with a reversal of Congress and state legislatures abrogating their legislative duties to the administrative agencies. Administrative regulations should be just that; details on administrative procedures such as application requirements, reporting, and other paperwork details. Rules beyond that level necessarily require a balancing decision, weighing intended benefits coming from a rule against the costs it will impose on government, consumers, and jobs. Single-purpose agencies are organizationally incapable of doing this balancing across the multiple interests these decisions will affect. Bureaucracies by their nature are similarly incapable of properly addressing what are fundamentally political decisions. This process is also undemocratic in that interest groups continue to promote their single interest goals through administrative regulations and lawsuits, knowing full well their chances are slim if instead decided in the legislative realm as required by the Constitution.

Where these rules affect the type and availability of jobs, they affect people's job prospects, the future of our economy, and future revenues to fund federal programs. Congress should not duck these hard decisions by simply passing them off to the agencies. They should instead be the final decision maker on major policy decisions.

## OCCUPATIONAL LICENSING

One of the most pernicious barriers to upward mobility continues to be the maze of rules and fees associated with occupational licensing. Preparing for and securing a license for many is the most immediate means to upgrade their skills, increase their wages, and in many instances, start a small business. But occupational licensing is hampered by different rules in every state and even within many states, different rules in cities and counties. Someone moving to gain greater income opportunities risks the prospect of being unable to conduct their trade, and is faced with the often high cost of meeting another set of rules, applications, and fees that do not change what they're able to do, only what government allows them to do.

This is not a new problem. Occupational licensing—in this instance for taxis—was used to combat boycotts organized by Martin Luther King in Baton Rouge and Montgomery,[116] and for long periods was used to restrict who could engage in certain trades. Even the Obama Administration acknowledged that this was an area where regulation has gone too far.

Yet while licensing can bring benefits, current systems of licensure can also place burdens on workers, employers, and consumers, and too often are inconsistent, inefficient, and arbitrary. The evidence suggests that licensing restricts mobility across states, increases the cost of goods and services to consumers, and reduces access to jobs in licensed occupations. The employment barriers created by licensing may raise wages for those who are successful in gaining entry to a licensed occupation, but they also raise prices for consumers and limit opportunity for other workers in terms of both wages and employment. By one estimate, licensing restrictions cost millions of jobs nationwide and raise consumer expenses by over one hundred billion dollars. The barriers imposed by licensing can prevent workers from succeeding in the best job for them, which in turn makes our labor market less efficient and ultimately can limit economic growth.[117]

Despite these long debates, this anti-competitive and anti-opportunity system continues today, but should be treated as what it truly is—an impermissible restraint to interstate commerce and an archaic system having disparate impacts on those least able to afford it as they seek to improve their wages and income by moving within the U.S. Reform is especially important to help people who have lost their jobs or been furloughed as a result of the coronavirus-related recession to earn a living from home and provide for their families.

Under a K-14 system, the current system of occupational licensing should be replaced with certificates/licensing earned through an associate's degree, including as necessary any experience to be obtained through a companion apprenticeship. Once earned through a certified K-14 system, reciprocity should be automatic, and the holders should be allowed to practice their trade anywhere within the U.S.

## CREATE A VENTURE-CAPITAL CULTURE

The federal agencies are now largely centralized in and around Washington, with government workers spending most of their days talking to other government workers and lobbyists rather than the employers and workers their rules and programs affect and researchers looking for opportunities to take their work beyond the bench stage. Regional offices do exist, but their communications stream is directed to Washington rather than the broader economy where they work.

To help create a venture capital culture for other industries, a number of the federal departments should be relocated to different parts of the heartland, preferably to urban areas in need of revitalization as a result of past or looming economic dislocation. For example, Transportation could go to Detroit. Health broken off from Health and Human Services to reshape an organizational culture centered around welfare and moved to upstate New York. Commerce to Chicago. Energy to the Southwest. Agriculture to the Midwest or Southeast. Interior to Denver or Salt Lake City. In this way, existing federal funding can be used to create the conditions for new centers of growth for other industries in our economy.

Along with the physical moves, a portion of budgets—taken from existing research funds for ongoing activities plus an additional 5 to 10 percent assessment on each program as seed funding—should also be moved to create related, interconnected research centers in local and regional universities, with the specific charge to advance the related industries and the jobs they provide and can provide to our economically lagging regions.

This type of research-business consortia that now exists for high tech was once a more common feature in leaders of the traditional industries, for example Bell Laboratories and Kodak Research Laboratories. Through these centers, conduits were created to direct basic research immediately into commercialization. But as our industrial structure was changed and as many are now under competitive challenge from the technology disruptors, much of this resource has been sacrificed or severely reduced. This model worked in the past; it is working now in high tech. Government can play a role in relaunching centers of innovation to benefit other jobs as well and create the conditions to attract the venture capital other countries now maintain for these middle-class wage jobs.

## REMOVE THE POVERTY SHACKLES

The Earned Income Tax Credit as it is currently structured is tied to work and work as determined by earned income through a W-2 or 1099s. Phased out as earned income rises, it has a lower effective marginal tax rate to discourage upward mobility. But that tax is still there, and it is only one component on top of every other assistance program in place with their far larger disincentives to personal and family growth.

No efforts to improve skills, wage, and income opportunities can succeed as long as these programs continue as they have. We have more than fifty years of experience in this country with how they have kept an eighth of our people enslaved. We do not need fifty years more particularly now when they are beginning to encroach on the middle class as well.

The negative income tax as first conceived was closer to a free market approach. It was proposed not as an addition, but as a replacement for the maze of poverty programs, their rules, administrative costs, uncertainty, and destruction of personal initiative and hope. We should return to this concept and replace the current programs to the extent possible with an expanded EITC. This shift will not remove the program disincentives entirely, but they will bring them to the minimum level that likely can be achieved.

To counter any tendency to use an expanded EITC as the back door to enact a UBI, this approach should not be authorized for more than five years at a time. Pegging the benefit level to the unemployment rate should also be an option to consider.

The program savings from substantially reduced administrative costs should be redirected into block grants to the states to implement the K-14 reforms. The amount of potential funding from this approach has been estimated in the general range of 5 to 6 percent for the federal agencies. The California research indicates the state and local take is about the same.[118] Using this component can help drive the political imperative to shift these programs into a more useful form. It also provides a clear connection by taking funds that now keep the poor in place and using it to once again give them hope.

More than a free market concept, there is also a political purpose to this approach. Congress does not react to spending. Prior measures to bring the federal deficit under control were thrown to the fiscal winds since the 2008-09 Great Recession. Spending is seen as bringing something home to the state and the district. It is why the poverty programs have continued to expand their size and reach even as they have failed in their fundamental job.

Congress, however, does respond to revenues, and EITC is at its base a revenue measure. If the poor and working poor are increasing, Congress will have less revenue to spend. And if they have less revenue, there will be a clear incentive to do what is needed to get those poor and working poor back to work, including control of regulations that would otherwise affect their jobs.

More critically, this approach would get the poor out of the agency maze that now dominates their lives and bring them into the world of work, taxes, and outrage over misplaced spending with which the rest of us now have to contend. It would reshape their focus to developing job skills, not the skills required to survive in a government web.

## LIFTING THE BARRIERS TO HOME OWNERSHIP

Owning your home remains the primary if not dominant source of wealth for families in the middle and lower income ranges. The plunge in home values at the start of the Great Recession consequently was felt most strongly by these groups. Policies designed to help them walk away instead of staying in their homes destroyed those wealth gains forever. Public policies that continue to limit the supply of new construction mean far too many are now priced out of the chance to ever rebuild it.

As shown in Federal Reserve System data,[119] homeownership rates have slowly recovered since that period, but not at the income levels that need it the most as a source of generational mobility. These groups instead increasingly have been relegated by public policy into a course designed to turn them into a perpetual renting class. Solutions to supply shortages are defined in terms of only affordable and public housing. The all-too-frequent answer to rising prices is a lurch to rent control that degrades the housing stock in the long run rather than supply expansion that would provide lasting benefits.

There are a number of steps that should be taken to expand housing overall, bring prices back under control, and restore the ability of housing to function as a means towards upward mobility. Federal policies should promote more housing supply and create mechanisms to expand ownership.

Lower income buyer assistance typically has relied on ever higher subsidies, but these do nothing other than raise the federal debt unless actions are first taken to increase supply. Federal housing assistance should shift from building rentals to building units for sale. Much like extensive federal grants in the 1960s and 1970s to build water, sewer, roads, and other infrastructure made middle class housing more affordable and more available, current funding should be shifted to this purpose and counter the current practice of local governments to raise development costs through high building and "impact" fees.

Federal assistance to the states related to housing and infrastructure should not be used to subsidize the growing cost premiums coming from high regulation. Existing funding should be conditioned on the states reforming their rules to enable adequate housing of their populations. Caps on allowable total cost per unit should apply to Community Development Block Grant and other HUD affordable housing funds as well as the Low-Income Housing Tax Credits that now form the primary source of funding for this purpose. At least some of federal transportation funds should be covered as well, starting with public transit funds going only to cities that have reformed their rules to enable market rate housing for people who would actually start riding these systems. States should be free to adopt the regulations they want, but the rest of the country should not be expected to pick up the bill for the resulting costs.

Home buying assistance currently concentrates on first-time buyers. The reality for many in the lower income ranges, however, is that their financial circumstances change. They may be forced to go through periods where for cost reasons they must go back to renting. More important, they may have opportunities for better wages and incomes if they move to a new area. Home buying assistance should not be entirely open-ended but flexible.

There should also be more instruments to provide this assistance but pegged to better supply. Similar to tax-preferred accounts for portable benefits, measures should be created to promote savings for down payments. Another measure more in line with the concept of tax equity has been proposed as the Low-income First Time Homebuyer (LIFT Home) tax credit,[120] under which buyers with incomes below 80 percent of median income would have the option of foregoing the interest deduction in return for a one-time refundable tax credit, shifting tax policy from promoting debt to promoting household capital.

# CONCLUSION

One only need to turn on the nightly news to be reminded that American politics is divisive. The fact is this is not a new phenomenon. American politics has been divisive from day one. There have been great debates in the founding of the nation, including but not limited to the question of slavery.

I often hear people say that we have lost our way or we no longer know how to compromise. Some of that may be true, but I suspect the greater cause of what ails America today is that entire generations feel left out of the promise of a better life that our country has always offered to those who were willing to work hard, play by the rules, and take the long view.

My grandparents could have never thought of affording dinner at the famed Tavern on the Green in New York City's Central Park. But two generations later, I have the resources to take my daughter to dinner there. This type of story repeats itself over and again in America. But for too many people, the hope and aspiration of upward economic mobility is fading and is being replaced with the stress of managing an ever-increasing cost of living that forces people to live paycheck to paycheck.

Based on the economic resurgence we experienced in more normal times before the COVID-19 crisis, why do so many people feel left behind?

The truth is that American policymakers have let people down. They promised students big loans for education without fully explaining the costs of those loans, and when and how to use them to get ahead. They promised working poor people help in the form of welfare that only limited their future, instead of expanding it. They guaranteed home ownership to later bail out the big banks and not the working families who lost everything in the Great Recession. And the promises of progressive politicians for free education and free health care are nothing more than the same empty lies of the past.

The simple truth is that many Americans feel the American Dream has passed them by and is unattainable. They are no longer vested in America because they do not see a path for their own advancement or that of their families. Therein has been America's greatest promise—not just individual opportunity, but generational wealth creation so that a grandparents' sacrifices would lead to greater and greater assimilation and upward economic mobility for the generations that followed.

We need to stop thinking about giving away free things that only enslave and hold people down. The War on Poverty and the massive expansion of the welfare state under Obama showed that government handouts can only provide a modest safety net—one that ends up setting a ceiling, not a floor for generational wealth creation. These programs trap and enslave generations. They always have and always will because in the name of equalizing the playing field, everyone but the super wealthy are held back, not helped up by the system. This is a false elixir and sadly too many politicians today use it to pander for votes.

Instead, we need to understand that the nature of work has changed and build a new social safety net – one not built for the 1940s and 1950s but one imagined for the next century. This is the time for a skills-based education network that extends beyond K-12 and prepares people for meaningful work through vocational training and higher education. We need to facilitate more opportunity with a growing economy and reforms that eliminate barriers, like overly oppressive licensure requirements that protect the haves from the have nots.

The workplace needs to be reimagined for people who do not stay at the same company for a lifetime but move from opportunity to opportunity as they grow and enhance their skills and their interests. Benefits need to be portable and vested to the person, not the employer. Let workers pick a retirement plan, a health care plan, a home savings plan and an education savings plan… and let employers fund those personal plans as workers move in and out of employment.

To make this all work, we need an educated workforce which in and of itself demands education reforms that improve school performance, not just the pay and benefits of those who work in schools. If education is the path out of poverty as I think it is, then we must demand better performance at teaching and focus on raising people up. School choice, vouchers, and performance standards all have a place in helping people trapped in underperforming schools escape their condition.

Every step of my life proves these points. I was born poor and would have stayed poor like the generations before me if it were not for the courage of my mother to not accept help. Instead, she sacrificed by leaving me behind, going to college, building a career and finding real independence outside of government assistance. She then paved the way for me to take school more seriously, attend college and build my own career.

In doing so, I've worked for others and built my own businesses two and three times over. The benefits of a job vested with an employer did not hold me back. Today, my benefits follow me because I've funded different accounts that provide real independence and liberty. Everyone should benefit from this type of security and mobility.

My daughters will grow up in a different place and time than I. They will have even more opportunity because we have broken the cycle of generational dependence. We need all Americans to be vested in America... and feel the same hope, share the same opportunity, and provide for their families as best meets their needs. I envision a system that encourages, rewards, and empowers people.

---

*Some portions of this book adapted from previous articles by Damon Dunn and from "My Rise from Poverty and Why Socialism Doesn't Work," Pacific Research Institute Issue Brief, August 2019.*

# ENDNOTES

1       Congressional Research Service, "Federal Spending on Benefits and Services for People with Low Income: In Brief," February 6, 2018.

2       Robert Rector and Vijay Menon, "Understanding the Hidden $1.1 Trillion Welfare System and How to Reform It," The Heritage Foundation, Backgrounder No. 3294, April 5, 2018.

3       Accessed through https://beta.sam.gov/.

4       Vision Strategy & Insights, "Barriers to Economic Development in California, Quantitative Research Study," Summary Report, 2017.

5       Congressional Budget Office, "Effective Marginal Tax Rates for Low- and Moderate-Income Workers," November 2012; "Effective Marginal Tax Rates for Low- and Moderate-Income Workers in 2016," November 2015.

6       Elaine Maag, C. Eugene Steuerle, Ritadhi Chakravarti, Caleb Quakenbush, "How Marginal Tax Rates Affect Families at Various Levels of Poverty," *National Tax Journal*, December 12, 2012.

7       California Business Roundtable, "Policy Recommendations: Jobs, Poverty & Upward Mobility," May 2018.

8       Sir Thomas More, *Utopia*, London: Cassell and Company, Limited, 1909.

9       Juan Luis Vives, *On Assistance to the Poor*, translated by Alice Tobriner, Toronto: University of Toronto Press, 1999.

10      J.E. King and John Marangos, "Two Arguments for Basic Income: Thomas Paine (1737-1809) and Thomas Spence (1750-1814)," *History of Economic Ideas*, Vol. XIX, No. 1, 2006.

11      Ibid.

12      Ibid.

13      Karl Polanyi, *The Great Transformation*, Boston: Beacon Press Books, 2001, p. 82.

14      Ibid.

15      Karl Polanyi, *The Great Transformation*, Boston: Beacon Press Books, 2001, p. 83-4, footnote omitted.

16    Boyer, George, "English Poor Laws," EH.Net Encyclopedia, edited by Robert Whaples. May 7, 2002. URL http://eh.net/encyclopedia/english-poor-laws/.

17    See for a summary of the criticisms, Rutger Bregman, "Nixon's Basic Income Plan," *Jacobin*, June 5, 2016.

18    Betrand Russell, *The Proposed Roads to Freedom*, London: Unwin Books, 1918, pp. 80-81.

19    Larry DeWitt, "The Townsend Plan's Pension Scheme, Research Note #17," Virginia Commonwealth Social Welfare History Project, December 2001.

20    Huey Long, "Share the Wealth, Every Man a King," pamphlet, 1934.

21    C.H. Douglas, *Social Credit*, London: Eyre and Spottiswoode, 1924, revised 1933.

22    E. Mabel & Dennis Milner, "Scheme for a State Bonus: A Rational Method of Solving the Social Problem," pamphlet printed by North of England Newspaper co., Ltd., June 1918.

23    George D.H. Cole, *Money, Its Present and Future*, London: Cassell and Company Ltd., 1944; *A History of Socialist Thought, Volume I, The Forerunners 1789-1850*, London: MacMillan & Co., 1953.

24    James Edward Meade, *Agathopia: The Economics of Partnership, Aberdeen*: Aberdeen University Press, 1989.

25    George J. Stigler, "The Economics of Minimum Wage Legislation," *The American Economic Review*, June 1946.

26    Paul Samuelson, et al., A Statement by Economists on Income Guarantees and Supplements, *New York Times*, May 27, 1968..

27    Alicia H. Munnell, Ed., "Lessons from the Income Maintenance Experiments," Federal Reserve Bank of Boston, Conference Series 30, September 1986.

28    Martin Luther King, Jr., *Where Do We Go from Here, Chaos or Community?*, Boston: Beacon Press, 1968, 1986, pp. 183-184.

29    Charles A. Murray, *In Our Hands: A Plan to Replace the Welfare State*, Washington, DC: The AEI Press, revised and updated edition, 2016.

30    Ad Hoc Committee on the Triple Revolution, "The Triple Revolution: Cybernation, Weaponry, Human Rights," March 1964.

31    Timothy Leary, *The Italians Chirp Like Happy Birds . . .*, letter, Mondo 2000, Number 6, 1992.

32    Jeremy S. Bluhm, *Are You Kidding, George? $1,000 a Person?*, The Harvard Crimson, June 14, 1973.

33    Hillary Rodham Clinton, *What Happened*, New York: Simon & Shuster, 2017, p. 239.

34    Liz Peek, "Gillibrand's Jobs Plan Another Federal Program We Don't Need," *The Hill*, April 23, 2018

35    "Jobs and an Economy for All," https://berniesanders.com/issues/jobs-for-all/.

36    Senator Kamala Harris, "Harris Proposes Bold Relief for Families Amid Rising Costs of Living," press release, October 18, 2018.

37    Andrew Yang 2020, "What is the Freedom Dividend?," accessed November 23, 2019.

38    Alicia H. Munnell, Ed., "Lessons from the Income Maintenance Experiments," Federal Reserve Bank of Boston, Conference Series 30, September 1986.

39    Kathleen Pender, "Oakland Group Plans to Launch Nation's Biggest Basic-Income Research Project," *San Francisco Chronicle*, September 21, 2017.

40    Kori Hale, "Universal Basic Income Comes To California With $500 Monthly Upgrade," *Forbes*, October 18, 2019.

41    Benjamin Kentish, "Hawaii Considering Universal Basic Income after Positive Trials in Europe," *Independent*, September 5, 2017.

42    Brad Jones, "We Could See an Indian Universal Basic Income by 2020," *Futurism*, January 31, 2018.

43    Chris Weller, "The Largest Basic Income Experiment in History is Coming to Kenya," *Business Insider*, April 18, 2016.

44    Rachel Sharp, "Universal Basic Income Around the World," *HR Magazine*, February 2019.

45      Tracy Brown Hamilton, "The Netherlands' Upcoming Money-for-Nothing Experiment," *The Atlantic*, June 21, 2016.

46      Adam O'Neal, "Italy Institutes a Universal Basic Income. Is the U.S. Next?," *Wall Street Journal*, February 27, 2019.

47      Jonathan Watts, "Brazil's Bolsa Familia Scheme Marks a Decade of Pioneering Poverty Relief," *The Guardian*, December 17, 2013.

48      Gretchen Frazee, "Ontario is Canceling its Basic Income Experiment," PBS, August 6, 2018.

49      Karin Olli-Nilsson, "Finland is Killing Its Experiment with Basic Income," *Business Insider*, April 19, 2018.

50      "Switzerland's Voters Reject Basic Income Plan," BBC News, June 5, 2016.

51      Citizen's Basic Income Feasibility Study Steering Group, "Assessing the Feasibility of Citizen's Basic Income Pilots in Scotland: An Interim Report," October 2019.

52      David Green, "Taiwan's Basic Income Movement Plans National Referendum," *The News Lens*, March 19, 2018.

53      Bryan Anderson, "Stockton's Mayor Doesn't Like Andrew Yang's Universal Basic Income Plan. Here's Why," *Sacramento Bee*, October 10, 2019.

54      Martin Luther King, Jr., *Where Do We Go from Here, Chaos or Community?*, Boston: Beacon Press, 1968, 1986, pp. 183-184.

55      Thomas Piketty, *Capital in the Twenty-First Century*, Harvard University Press, 2014; Thomas Piketty and Emmanuel Saez, "Income Inequality in the United States," 1913-1998, *The Quarterly Journal of Economics*, February 2003.

56      Max Ghenis, "Distributional Analysis of Andrew Yang's Freedom Dividend," UBI Center, June 24, 2019.

57      Kyle Pomerleau, "Does Andrew Yang's 'Freedom Dividend' Proposal Add Up?," Tax Foundation, July 24, 2019.

58      University of Pennsylvania, Penn Wharton Budget Model, *Options of Universal Basic Income: Dynamic Modeling*, March 29, 2018.

59      Alexis de Tocqueville, *Democracy in America, Volume Two*, Part Four, Chapter VI: What Sort of Despotism Democratic Nations Have to Fear, 1840.

60    California Business Roundtable, "Jobs, Poverty and Upward Mobility," 2019.

61    Ibid.

62    US Census Bureau, "The Supplemental Poverty Measure: 2018," September 10, 2019. Note that the Census Bureau has indicated that errors in their published estimates are currently being revised. Data in this report is based on the unrevised data as released with the September 2019 report.

63    California Business Roundtable, "Policy Recommendations: Jobs, Poverty & Upward Mobility," May 2018.

64    Federal Reserve definition of "family" is closer to the Census Bureau definition for "household" rather than "family."

65    This data point was not available for Houston and San Antonio MSAs. The value for the core county in each case was used instead.

66    Federal Reserve Bank of St. Louis (FRED), "Economic Research, 30-Year Fixed Rate Mortgage Average in the United States."

67    Citing information from studies by UC Berkeley's Terner Center for Housing Innovation and UC Berkeley School of Law, Jennifer Hernandez, "California Environmental Quality Act Lawsuits and California's Housing Crisis," Hastings Environmental Law Journal, Vol. 24, Number 1, Winter 2018, estimates that in California mid-rise apartments cost 2.5 times per square foot higher to construct than single homes. High-rise apartment construction cost is about twice as high on a square foot basis than mid-rise.

68    Wayne Winegarden, Ph.D., *Legislating Energy Prosperity*, Pacific Research Institute, May 2020.

69    Wayne Winegarden, Ph.D., *Legislating Energy Poverty*, Pacific Research Institute, December 2018.

70    US Environmental Protection Agency, Inventory of U.S. Greenhouse Gas Emissions and Sinks: 1990-2017, 2019.

71    California Air Resources Board, 2000-2017 GHG Emissions Trends and Indicators Report, 2019.

72    Wayne Winegarden, Ph.D., *Costly Subsidies for the Rich*, Pacific Research Institute, February 2018.

73    Wendell Cox, "Employment Access in US Metropolitan Areas (2017)," *NewGeography*, November 23, 2018.

74    Wayne Winegarden, Ph.D., *Legislating Energy Prosperity*, Pacific Research Institute, May 2020.

75    For additional detail, see California Center for Jobs & the Economy, California Affordability Index.

76    Sources include:  US Bureau of Labor Statistics, "Current Employment Statistics"; US Bureau of Labor Statistics, "Employment by Industry, 1910 and 2015," March 3, 2016; Dorothy S. Brady, ed., "Output, Employment, and Productivity in the United States after 1800, "National Bureau of Economic Research, 1966; US Census Bureau, "Historical Statistics of the United States, 1789-1945," 1949.

77    Carl Benedikt Frey and Michael A. Osborne, *The Future of Employment: How Susceptible are Jobs to Computerisation?*, Oxford Martin School, September 2013.

78    Susan Lund, James Manyika, Liz Hilton Segel, André Dua, Bryan Hancock, Scott Rutherford, and Brent Macon, "The Future of Work in America," McKinsey and Company, July 2019; James Manyika, Susan Lund, Michael Chui, Jacques Bughin, Jonathan Woetzel, Parul Batra, Ryan Ko, and Saurabh Sanghvi, "Jobs Lost, Jobs Gained:  Workforce Transitions in a Time of Automation," McKinsey and Company December 2017; James Manyika, Michael Chui, Mehdi Miremadi, Jacques Bughin, Katy George, Paul Willmott, and Martin Dewhurst, "A Future that Works:  Automation, Employment, and Productivity," McKinsey and Company, January 2017.

79    Karl Marx, (translated by Martin Nicolaus), *Grundrisse:  Foundations of the Critique of Political Economy* (1857-8), Penguin Classics, 1993.

80    Author's calculations using US Bureau of Labor Statistics, Average Hourly Earnings of Production and Nonsupervisory Employees and CPI-W.

81    Author's calculations using US Bureau of Labor Statistics, Average Hourly Earnings of Production and Nonsupervisory Employees and US Bureau of Economic Analysis, PCE Index.

82    Donald J. Boudreaux, *The Myth of American Middle-Class Stagnation*, American Institute for Economic Research, July 29, 2019.

83    Mary C. Daly, Bart Hobijn, and Benjamin Pyle, "What's Up with Wage Growth?," Federal Reserve Bank of San Francisco Economic Letter, March 7, 2016.

84    These numbers only address wages. The more recent CBO study, "The Effects on Employment and Family Income of Increasing the Federal Minimum Wage," July 2019, also looked at the effect of a $15 federal minimum wage on costs.

85    For example, see Thomas Mroz and Timothy Savage, "The Long-Term Effects of Youth Unemployment," Employment Policies Institute, October 2001 and Paul Gregg and Emma Tominey, "The Wage Scar From Male Youth Unemployment," Labour Economics, August 2005.

86    Congressional Budget Office, "The Effects of a Minimum-Wage Increase on Employment and Family Income," February 18, 2014.

87    Congressional Budget Office, "The Effects on Employment and Family Income of Increasing the Federal Minimum Wage," July 2019.

88    Bureau of Labor Statistics Research CPI-U, allowing for comparison of costs over a longer time frame.

89    Educational Attainment in the 1970 Census was measured by number of years of school completed. The figure takes 4 years of college as equivalent to earning a BA. High school diploma includes GED or equivalent. Some college includes persons holding an AA.

90    US Bureau of Labor Statistics, "National Occupational Employment and Wage Estimates," May 2018.

91    US Census Bureau, "2018 American Community Survey," Median Owner Housing Costs of $18,792.

92    United Auto Workers Research, "Taking the High Road: Strategies for a Fair EV Future," Spring 2019.

93    US Bureau of Labor Statistics, "Highlights of the May 2017 Data on Electronically Mediated Work," recoded data, September 28, 2018.

94    White, African-American, and Asian may be of any ethnicity; Latinos may be any race.

95    Assembly Bill 5 (Chapter 296, California Statutes of 2019).

96    Alan Greenspan, *The Age of Turbulence*, New York: The Penguin Press, 2007.

97    Claudia Goldin & Lawrence F. Katz, *The Race Between Education and Technology*, Cambridge, Massachusetts: The Belknap Press of Harvard University Press, 2008.

98    Paul Beston, "When High Schools Shaped America's Destiny," *City Journal*, The Shape of Work to Come, 2017.

99    Jay P. Greene, "GEDs Aren't Worth the Paper They're Printed On," *City Journal*, Winter 2002.

100   Jackson Toby, 'Free College for All' Is an Experiment That Has Already Failed, *Wall Street Journal*, December 7-8, 2019.

101   CBS Los Angeles, California Will Pay 2 Years of Community College Tuition For First-Time Students, August 29, 2019.

102   California Legislative Analyst's Office, "Overview of Tuition-Free Community College Programs," February 3, 2016; Ashley A. Smith, "Survey: Non-Tuition Expenses Hinder California College Students," *EdSource*, September 13, 2019.

103   California Legislative Analyst's Office, EdBudget Figures, K-12 Funding by Source.

104   The Campaign for College Opportunity, "The Transfer Maze: The High Cost to Students and the State of California," September 2017.

105   Paul Beston, "When High Schools Shaped America's Destiny," *City Journal*, The Shape of Work to Come, 2017.

106   Fermin Leal, "Summer Remedial Courses Now Required for Nearly Half of CSU Freshmen," *EdSource*, August 9, 2015.

107   Alexei Koseff, "CSU Eliminates Remedial Classes in Push to Improve Graduation Rates," *Sacramento Bee*, August 3, 2017."

108   Grover J. "Russ" Whitehurst, *Can We Be Hard-Headed About Preschool? A Look at Head Start*, Brookings Institution, The Brown Center Chalkboard Series Archive, January 16, 2013.

109   Henry Fernandez, "Trump Administration Expands Pre-tax Accounts for Health Insurance Coverage," Fox Business News, June 14, 2019.

110   Joyce M. Rosenberg, "New Law May Encourage Businesses to Offer Retirement Plans," Associated Press, January 5, 2020.

111   Assembly Bill 5 (Chapter 296, California Statutes of 2019).

112   Steven Hsieh, "Seattle City Council Passes New Labor Standards for Domestic Workers," *Curbed Seattle*, July 23, 2018.

113    HB 1601 – 2019-20, Creating the Universal Worker Protections Act, Washington State Legislature.

114    Pension Rights Service, *State-based Retirement Plans for the Private Sec*tor, updated May 2016.

115    Clyde Wayne Crews, Jr., "Trump's Year in Regulation, 2019," *Forbes*, December 31, 2019.

116    Timothy Sandefur, "Can You Get There from Here?: How The Law Still Threatens King's Dream," *Law & Equality*, Vo. 22, 2004.

117    The White House, "Occupational Licensing: A Framework for Policymakers," July 2015, pp. 7-8.

118    California Center for Jobs & the Economy, "California Public Assistance Programs & Upward Mobility," February 2018.

119    Federal Reserve System, Survey of Consumer Finances, Internal Data Series.

120    Edward J. Pinto, "Market-Based Solutions are the Only Way to Get Home Prices and Rents Back in Line," AEIdeas, AEI, July 18, 2016.

# ACKNOWLEDGEMENTS

I would like to thank several people for their help in writing this book: Michael Kahoe for his command of the data, understanding of complicated policy issues, and ability to provide meaningful insight into numerous drafts and revisions; Eddy Cremata for his excellent research and working with me to shape the voice of this book project; The California Center for Jobs and the Economy which provides an objective and definitive source of information pertaining to job creation and economic trends in the United States; Dana Beigel for her wonderful design and Sally Pipes, President and CEO of the Pacific Research Institute, for agreeing to publish the book.

# ABOUT THE AUTHOR

DAMON DUNN is a fellow in Business and Economics at the Pacific Research Institute. He writes the twice monthly "Free Markets 101" column for PRI's *Right by the Bay* blog.

Dunn is a successful real estate developer, investor and businessman, former collegiate and pro football player, and was a Hoover Institution fellow from 2011-13.

He is the founder and managing member of Lagunita Industries, LLC., a company that acquires and grows privately-held businesses with annual cash flows between $2 million and $5 million. The company has been capitalized by a Los Angeles-based family office with a significant base of permanent capital and a very long-term investment horizon.

Prior to its founding, he was president and a principal owner of The Tricor Companies, a real estate investment firm that invested and developed retail projects nationwide. Under his leadership, The Tricor Companies completed 28 retail projects in excess of $160 million of aggregate value.

Dunn is a graduate of Stanford University with a B.A. in Public Policy.

# ABOUT PRI

The Pacific Research Institute (PRI) champions freedom, opportunity, and personal responsibility by advancing free-market policy solutions. It provides practical solutions for the policy issues that impact the daily lives of all Americans, and demonstrates why the free market is more effective than the government at providing the important results we all seek: good schools, quality health care, a clean environment, and a robust economy.

Founded in 1979 and based in San Francisco, PRI is a non-profit, non-partisan organization supported by private contributions. Its activities include publications, public events, media commentary, community leadership, legislative testimony, and academic outreach.

### CENTER FOR BUSINESS AND ECONOMICS

PRI shows how the entrepreneurial spirit—the engine of economic growth and opportunity—is stifled by onerous taxes, regulations, and lawsuits. It advances policy reforms that promote a robust economy, consumer choice, and innovation.

### CENTER FOR EDUCATION

PRI works to restore to all parents the basic right to choose the best educational opportunities for their children. Through research and grassroots outreach, PRI promotes parental choice in education, high academic standards, teacher quality, charter schools, and school-finance reform.

### CENTER FOR THE ENVIRONMENT

PRI reveals the dramatic and long-term trend toward a cleaner, healthier environment. It also examines and promotes the essential ingredients for abundant resources and environmental quality: property rights, markets, local action, and private initiative.

### CENTER FOR HEALTH CARE

PRI demonstrates why a single-payer Canadian model would be detrimental to the health care of all Americans. It proposes market-based reforms that would improve affordability, access, quality, and consumer choice.

### CENTER FOR CALIFORNIA REFORM

The Center for California Reform seeks to reinvigorate California's entrepreneurial self-reliant traditions. It champions solutions in education, business, and the environment that work to advance prosperity and opportunity for all the state's residents.

### CENTER FOR MEDICAL ECONOMICS AND INNOVATION

The Center for Medical Economics and Innovation aims to educate policymakers, regulators, health care professionals, the media, and the public on the critical role that new technologies play in improving health and accelerating economic growth.

CPSIA information can be obtained
at www.ICGtesting.com
Printed in the USA
FSHW010654030720

9 781934 276426